HARVESTING TRADITION

HARVESTING TRADITION

WRITTEN AND PRODUCED BY

BENJAMIN LESTER

RECIPES, ESSAYS, PHOTOGRAPHY,

LAYOUT, AND DESIGN BY BENJAMIN LESTER

WWW.LOCALGRAIN.ORG

Published by Farm Feast

A division of Wheatberry LLC

www.localgrain.org

Library of Congress Cataloging-in-Publication Data

Lester, Benjamin

Harvesting Tradition / by Benjamin Lester

p. cm.

ISBN 978-1-7343820-0-6

In loving Memory of

My Father, James Matthew Lester

and

For My Mother, Margaret Schoen Lester

TABLE OF CONTENTS

Other ways to connect with Ben and his work.

www.localgrain.org

is the home of Ben's Business Farm Feast

and where you can find Ben's recipes and videos.

It is also the place to sign up for Ben's Farm Share Programs:

The Pioneer Valley Heritage Grain CSA
The Farmer's Pantry Share
and The Rice Share

Ben can be contacted at Ben@localgrain.org
Please feel free to ask Ben questions about what you find at www.localgrain.org

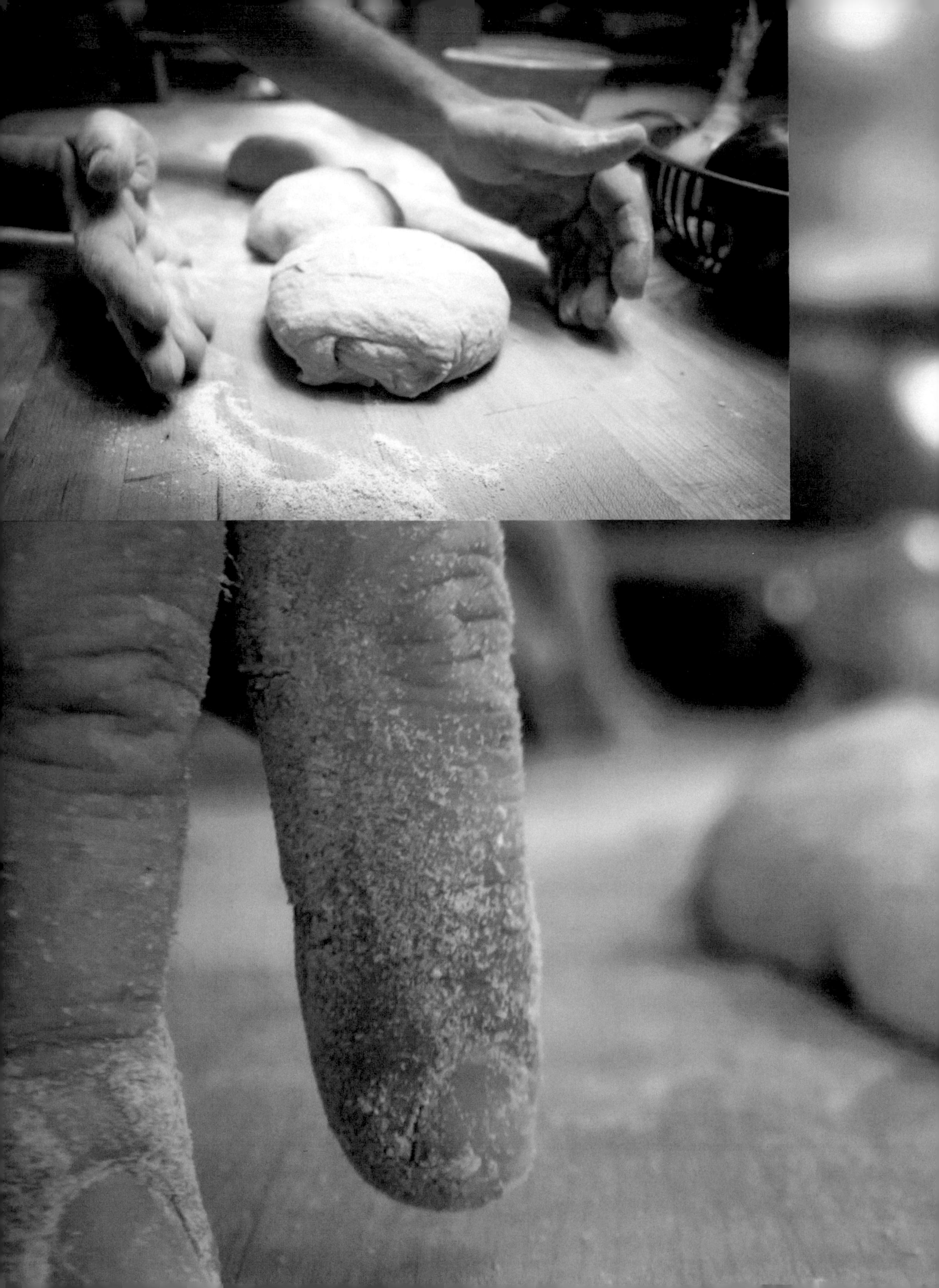

INTRODUCTION

"The Most Wonderful Story I know is, perhaps, that this bread, thousands of years old though it is, is not yet finished in the baking. Botanist, farmer, miller, and baker are still experimenting with it. The entire story of bread goes very deep-its social and technical, religious, political, and scientific story"

H.E JACOB "SIX THOUSAND YEARS OF BREAD"

Cooking and baking as we know it took over two million years of research and development as people and their traditions passed down from one generation to the next. The culinary traditions we take part in each and every day are not only what makes us human, but how humanity emerged nearly two million years ago.

I hope this book finds you hungry to learn about a variety of   mouthwatering and soul-nourishing, food traditions. This is our culinary heritage through the lens of our great grain traditions and the work I've been doing for the past 15 years. I have spent much of my life exploring the traditions from around the world that inspire me, and this book contains the cream of the crop from my experience and work. I hope my passion and joy comes through these recipes and stories and ignites your kitchen with fun, pleasure, and a greater sense of connection and enjoyment

The fruit of plants in the family Poaceae or Gramineae (grasses) are what we call cereals or grains. Heritage grains are as ancient and elemental to civilization as cooking is to humanity. We have found cooked einkorn starch on the teeth of neanderthals (turns out sapiens weren't the only cooking ape). Large stores of intact grain have been found in caves in Israel dating back over 20,000 years and on stone tools in Africa dating back over 100,000 years. With the release of Richard Wrngham's groundbreaking book on the origins of cooking in 2008, we now have a very different picture of our ancient origins than what we were taught in school. As Wrangham explains in Catching Fire, humans are "the cooking apes" and it is this adaptation that allowed humanity to emerge nearly 2 million years ago. It is one of the most essential and defining characteristics of humanity.

With this perspective, we can begin to fully appreciate the depth and breadth of our ancient and modern food traditions. Every time you cook and prepare your food, you are doing something deeply human.

THE ROLE OF COOKING TRADITIONS IN HUMAN EVOLUTION

4.5–1.9 MILLION YEARS AGO — **2.8 – 1.5 MILLION YEARS AGO** — **1.9 MILLION –143,000 YEARS AGO** —

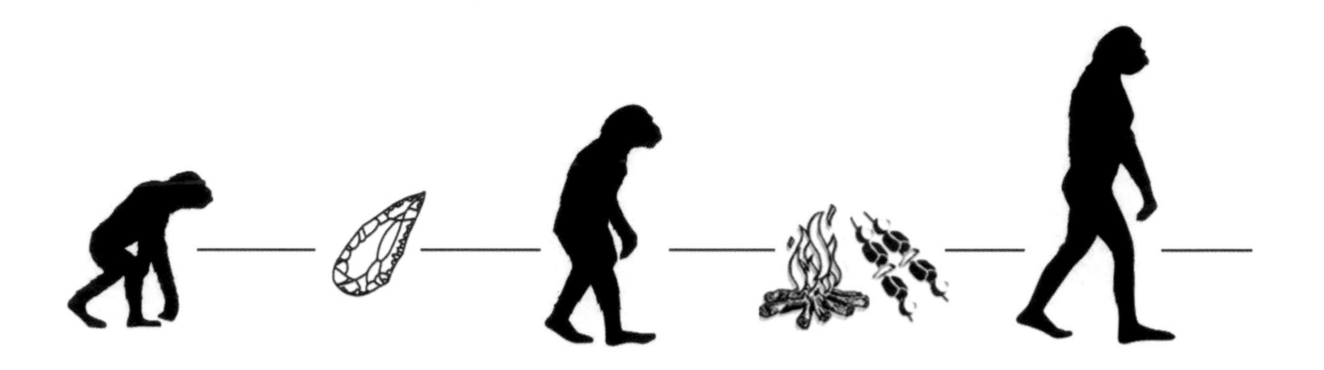

Austrolopithicus

Australopithecus ate an almost entirely raw food diet. The only access to cooked food for australopithecines would have been foraging in areas after a wildfire burned through, as many primates still do today.

These were also the first creatures to employ stone shards as knives. This was the primary catalyst of the evolution into Homo Habilis, who extensively made and used stone knives and other tools. They could now cut their meat and open bones to extract marrow as well as crush seeds, nuts, and tubers to ease digestion.

Homo Habilis

With their stone tools, improved mobility, and increased brain capacity, Homo Habilis would make one of the most catalyzing discoveries of mankind: that fire could be controlled and used to soften and preserve food Most importantly they got much more energy (about twice) from the same available foods.

This allowed metabolic energies to shift from big mouths, jaws, teeth and guts needed to chew and digest raw foods to shrink in favor of much bigger brains and improved bipedalism.

Homo Erectus

As cooking techniques improved, more and more energy went in to ever-increasing brain sizes and smaller digestive systems. The erectus skeleton also showed continued development towards bipedalism, making them a great runner, hunter and gatherer.

Not only did their food taste better cooked and provide more energy, it also lasted longer. Raw meat that would have spoiled in a few hours could be cooked and probably became the first "jerky."

"Fossil evidence indicates that [the dependence on cooked food] arose not just tens of thousands of years ago, or even a few hundred thousand, but right back at the beginning of our time on earth, at the start of human evolution, by the habiline that became homo erectus...We should indeed pin our humanity on cooks."

Richard Wrangham - Anthropological Biologist, Harvard University
and author of the book Catching Fire - How Cooking Made Us Human

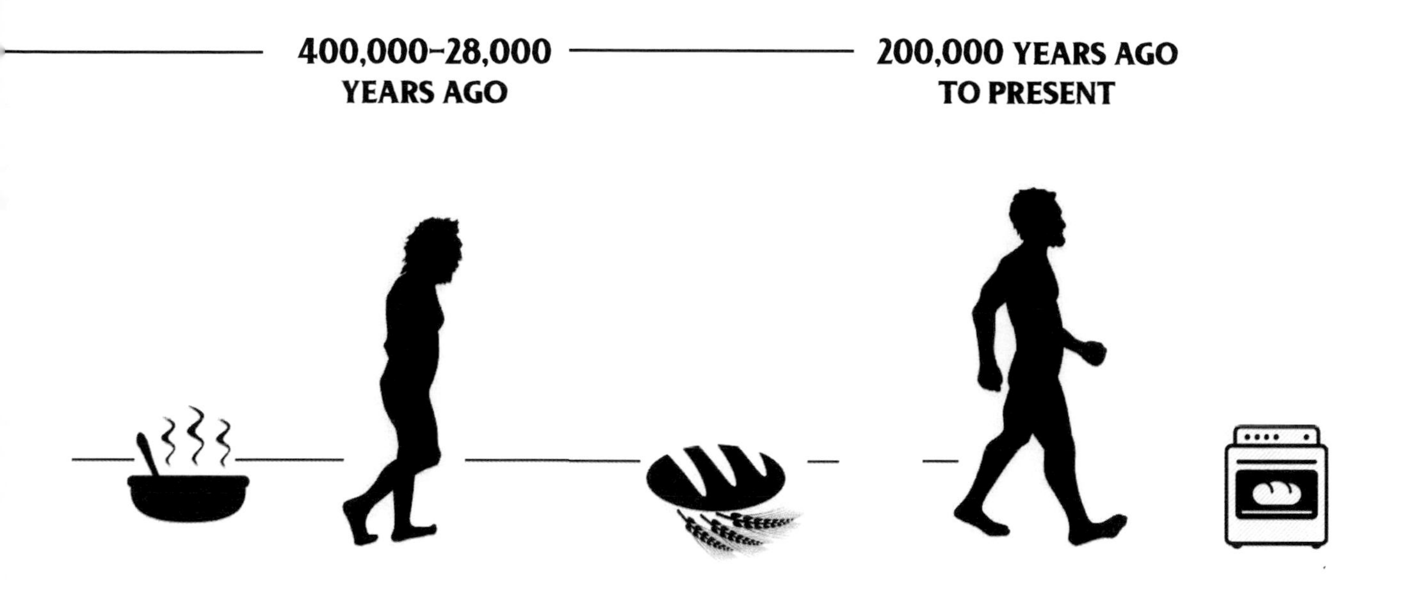

Homo Neandertalensis

While we are still working to uncover the details of the Neanderthal diet, we can gain some insights through examination of fossils. One 40,000-year old Neanderthal tooth had cooked einkorn in its dental calculus, showing that Neanderthals not only ate einkorn, but cooked it as well. Some leading archeologists believe there is evidence to suggest that neanderthals not only cooked with fire, but boiled some of their food in water, making the first soups and stews.

Homo Sapiens

We still don't have all the answers to many questions about our evolution, but one of the most important things right now is to identify the right questions to ask. If the control of fire and ability to cook foods were the primary catalyst in the evolution from habilis to erectus, we have to ask whether certain milestones in the cooking process catalyzed the evolution from erectus to Neanderthal and Sapiens. I propose this is likely the case, as few things have as much of an impact on one's body and mind than the foods we eat. Most species are largely defined by diet, and humans are no certainly exception. Perhaps it was the discovery of bread that created sapiens. I suspect we may have an answer to this question in the next 50 years.

*This graphic is not intended to suggest that evolution is a linear progresion since it is not but instead to show the relation ship bewteen evolutionary catalysts and the species they led to. Many species in the human lineage are not present here. We now know that genes even move horizontily between species. Nothing is linear.

14,400 Years of Bread and Beyond

A bread crumb was carbon dated to 14,400 years old at an ancient Natufian hearth site in the Black Desert.

In July of 2018, at an archeological site in the Black desert of Jordan, the world's oldest known bread crumb was discovered. An ancient tribe known as the Natufians were baking flatbreads made of wild einkorn, oats, barley, and club rush tubers on their hearth stones in the center of their dwellings where their fires burned. While this is the oldest bread that has been found, it is certainly not the first bread made by humans.

Previously, it was thought that the development of widespread farming and settlement about ten thousand years ago led to the creation of bread, but now we know it went the other way around. Breadmaking predates widespread human settlement by at least 3,000 years. The advantages of cultivating cereals for basic sustenance was a better way to survive and procreate than chasing seasonal wild fruits and animals that required regular moving of camps.

Evidence also shows that small-scale agriculture (gardening) dates back at least 23,000 years. The "dawn of agriculture," happened when gardening and animal husbandry became the clear winner in terms of providing more high quality food more consistently than hunting and gathering. This allowed for permanent settlement, massive increases in population, and the development of increasingly specialized trades and economies. Grains became the foundation of civilization, where we no longer had to chase the vagaries of seasons and weather. Farming cereals and legumes was absolutely essential; these harvests were the most "shelf stable" as they were inherently dry and resistant to bugs and mold for extended periods of time. These stores could be gathered, held onto and used during the leanest months of the year.

The same thing happened in Southeast Asia with the cultivation of rice, as well as in the Americas with the cultivation of maize (corn). Rye and buckwheat were critical in eastern Europe and Russia, as was sorghum and millet in Africa.

This charred bread crumb from the Naftufian fire site indicates that the creation of bread may have been a driving force to settle down and grow grains

It has been shown to be made from about 80% emmer with the rest a mix of wild oats, barley and club rush tubers.

NATUFIAN ANCIENT GRAIN FLATBREAD

Re-Creating The Oldest Known Bread in the World

Unlike all of the other recipes in this book, I didn't do this one in hopes that you will make it. Instead, I included it so that you had an opportunity to see it and put the place of bread in pre historical perspective. near descendants of this bread is to this day are still incredibly vital and important in the world, especially as far as cultural food traditions go.

While this bread can be made with just einkorn and a modern oven for simplicity's sake, here we will make the most authentic recreation possible. This will include Einkorn, oats, barley, and manioc starch, the four ingredients found in the natufian Bread (we will substitute manioc for club rush tubers). We will also bake this on a traditional stone hearth with a live fire to get the full experience!

They may have ground the grain by pounding it between stones dry and then added water. It is also possible that they soaked the grains in water first, making them much softer before grinding/pounding. Also, while dry seeds and flour are prone to blowing around, wet seeds stay in place as the dough begins to form immediately and holds things together throughout the process. Einkorn, the most glutenis of these ingredients, would have formed the sticky, elastic base to hold this all together, as it accounts for about 80 percent of the grain used.

Ingredients:

1 pound einkorn
3 ounces oats
3 ounces barley
2 ounces Club Rush Tubers(tapioca or potato are reasonable substitutes)
2 teaspoons sea salt
2 cups water

Directions:

1. Soak all your small grains for 24 hours in 4 cups of water
2. Grind your grains and tubers with knocking stones, a metate, or in a food processor.
3. Allow your dough to develop as much flavor and fermentation as you like. The longer it sits at warmer temperatures, the more tangy it will get.
4. Preheat your oven to 450 degrees 30 minutes before the bake.
5. If you are using an outdoor fire, place a 2-3 foot diameter stone in the center of a 4-5 foot fireplace.
6. Build a fire around three sides of the stone and preheat until the center of the stone is about 350-400 degrees.You can also build a fire on the hearth stone to speed up the preheating process. Monitor hearth temperature with an infrared thermometer. Alternatively, toss some flour on the stone to gauge the heat; when it browns after about a minute, it's ready to use.
7. Using flour to dust the outsides, stretch your dough into a thin wheel shape about an 1/4 inch thick.
8. Toss a small amount of flour on the hearth to prevent sticking and toss your flatbread onto the hearth. Cook until the dough is set and is well-browned.
9. If you are finding that your stone isn't getting hot enough, place a few hot coals on the stone for several minutes to add some heat to the surface.

FOUNDATIONAL GRAINS OF CIVILIZATION

WHEAT

Origins - History - Types - Qualities - Usage

The Ancient Wild Wheat Grasses of the Fertile Crescent

Einkorn - Eaten for at least 45,000 years by humans including neanderthals - Diploid Wheat - Triticum Monococcum -

The first wheat gathered, eaten and eventually cultivated by humans was einkorn. A wild grass growing in the regions between what is modern day Turkey, Iraq and Israel. Cooked Einkorn residue was found on the teeth of a neanderthal man who lived 45,000 years ago and recently a very large store of einkorn grains were found in a cave in Israel that date back 23,000 years.

Einkorn is a hulled wheat and that means that the seeds gathered by hand would have been rubbed/pounded between two rocks to remove the hulls at which point they could be eaten raw or parched on the hearth floor to double the energetic yield, or pounded further into a flour that would then be mixed with water to make a dough or cooking on the hearth.

Emmer -Tetraploid wheat - Triticum Dicoccum - Earliest archaeological findings from 8,800bce

The first "hard wheat" and the precursor to Durum wheat. Emmer is darker in color than most wheats and well suited to many types of preparations. From Flatbreads to pasta, beer and simply cooked whole until it has the desired tenderness emmer is a unique part of the wheat family. Often referred to as farro in america this is a misunderstanding of italian language. In Itialian Farro means ancient wheat and each ancient wheat has it's designation by size. Farro Piccolo refers to einkorn, Farro medio refers to emmer, and farro grande refers to spelt. If you are buying something called just "farro" it is probably spelt as this is the least expensive of the three. I would suggest buying from a less generic source.

Durum - Tetraploid wheat - Triticum Durum - First free threshing or hulless wheat dating back to 7000bc

Durum is a particularly hard wheat, earning its namesake "Durum", which means "hard" in Latin. Prized for its pasta-making qualities, it also sometimes finds its way into breadmaking, typically as a portion of the wheat flour combined with bread wheat for better rising properties. This wheat was selected specifically for its ability to shed its protective shell with ease, making it the first "free threshing wheat". Since it was easier to get from field to plate, it became very popular and is one of the most grown wheats today, second only to bread wheat.

Spelt - Tetraploid wheat - Trticum Spelta - Also from a cross between emmer and another wild grass - cultivation dates back approximately to 5000 bc

While not free threshing like durum, spelt has the best rising properties of the ancient wheats, making it one of the most widely cultivated wheat in Europe during the Middle Ages. Of all the ancient pre hexaploid wheats, Spelt is the most suited to bread making and is generally very versatile like bread wheat (triticum aestivum).

Khorasan Wheat - Tetraploid wheat - Tritiucm Turgidum ssp. turanicum

Not a lot is known of the origins of Khorasan wheat. It is nearly twice the size of other wheats and is free threshing. It's not currently in commercial production in the Northeast, but hopefully it will be soon.

Bread Wheat - Hexaploid wheat - Triticum Aestivum - Dating back to at least 300bce

This is the most widely cultivated wheat worldwide (95% of total wheat production) because of its free threshing, superior rising properties, and overall versatility. Red Lammas is an heirloom variety or cultivar of red winter bread wheat. Redeemer wheat is also a modern variety (cultivar) of red winter bread wheat. They are both triticum aestivum.

Other Categorizing Characteristics

Hard or Soft

This refers to the hardness or softness of the wheat. If you can dent it with your fingernail, it is soft; if you can't, then it is hard. Generally there is a correlation between hardness/softness and the rising properties of the wheat for bread, though this is not always the case.

Winter or Spring

This refers to the planting schedule. Winter wheats are actually planted in the fall, going dormant through the winter and awakening in the early spring for growth to the flowering stage. This indication has little to do with baking properties and more to do with agricultural requirements. In New England, most wheat is planted in the fall (winter wheat) to accomodate for the wetter, weedier conditions that prevail most years in the spring.

Red or White

Color is also fairly self-explanatory. Most wheats are mainly brown with reddish hues that range in color.. White wheat is primarily a modern attempt to select varieties that will appeal to the market demand for whiter foods, as whiteness is an indication of a high calorie/low fiber food that is easy to eat.

YEAST AND FERMENTATION TEMPERATURES

While the second half of this book delves into the creation, maintanence and use of wild yeast cultures(sourdough starter), the first half presents the use of commercially produced yeast. It is easier to use and makes a milder, less acidic flavor profile. All these recipes call for instant yeast and not active dry. Active dry is inferior in many ways and costs 40-80 times more. It's not like instant oats or instant polenta, quality has been sacrificed for expediency. Instant is the same micro organism in a superior form. Not only is it far less expensive, but it keeps much longer and performs far more consistently. Also, there is no need for proofing the yeast to see if it's still alive, because it always is! You have to buy 1 pound at a time for about five dollars. It costs the same as a few ounces of active dry. Twice as much active dry is needed by weight to make the same bread.

Now that you've got the right yeast, let's talk about the most important and often overlooked part of baking with yeast- Temperature! You must have a thermometer to monitor the temperature of your dough during fermentation and final proofing of the loaf. Small variations in temperature can lead to very different and undesireable results. If you don't know the temperature of your dough, it is quite likely to go off track. This will surprise you in unpleasant ways. Much like a brick loaf of bread that never rises properly. For instance, this can happen when your fermenation temperature goes below 76 degrees. Please do not skip this step as a thermometer is only fifteen dollars and it's essential.

There certainly are methods of dough fermentation that entail longer and colder temperatures. The French Bread recipe in this book capitolizes on this technique.

Golden Soft Einkorn Pita and Lamb Gyro p. 30

HERITAGE WHEAT TRADITIONS

FLATBREADS

FROM ANTIQUITY TO TODAY

GOLDEN SOFT EINKORN PITA

WITH KOFTA, TZATZIKI, TOMATO, ONION, AND FRESH HERBS

The golden, soft, yellow-hued flour from einkorn wheat makes incomparably delicious pita bread. Soft and warm right off the skillet or from the oven, it simply can't be beat. While this dough is a little more tender and sticky than a dough made from hard wheat, a little extra dusting flour when patting or rolling out into shape is all the extra care needed. Its incredible flavor and soft texture is well worth the minimal extra effort.

The most important consideration when baking pitas is not to overbake or underbake them. Since they are thin, it is fairly easy to overbake them. They should be just set at an internal temperature of 195-200 degrees. While you can certainly try to monitor using a thermometer, it can be difficult to get accurate readings since the bread is so thin. If they come out dry you over baked; if they are gooey they didn't go long enough. You should be able to get the hang of it with practice.

Ingredients:

1 pound and 4 ounces einkorn flour
2 teaspoons salt
½ teaspoon instant yeast
2 cups water

Directions:

1. Mix flour with salt and yeast
2. Mix water with dry ingredients into dough with spoon
3. Allow to rise at least 30 percent in volume before using

After the initial rise, limit further rising by refrigerating the dough. It should be kept in the fridge for up to a week.

4. Scoop 1/3 cup of dough and pat into a round, using plenty of flour for dusting.
5. Roll out to about 6-8 inches and ⅛-1/4 inch thick

Thicker pitas can be patted into shape with the palm of your hand. For thinner pitas, a rolling pin works best. Use plenty of flour when patting or rolling your dough so it doesn't get stuck. You can always brush off excess flour after baking.

6. Bake for about 2 minutes per side on a hot griddle, or in an oven at 500 degrees, or over some charcoal on the grill.

Tzatziki

This sauce is simple, yet stunning. It compliments the lamb and pita, creating a symphony of mouthwatering flavors like few others.

1 cup greek yogurt (yogurt drained in cheesecloth)
The juice of 1/3 lemon
1/2 cup diced, peeled, and seeded cucumber
1 tablespoon chopped fresh dill(or dried if you can't get fresh)
1 teaspoon salt
Pepper to taste

Lamb Kofta

For those unfamiliar with Kofta, it is basically ground meat with herbs, spices, onions, and garlic. on a stick for grilling.

1 pound ground lamb (any ground meat will work)
1 teaspoon Salt
1/4 teaspoon black pepper
2 cloves minced or pureed garlic
4 tablespoons minced or pureed onion
1 tablespoon chopped mint
1 pinch allspice
1 pinch cumin
1 teaspoon oregano

Ancient Emmer Pita

with Fire Roasted Lamb and Lemon Garlic Tahini Sauce

There's nothing like roasting and grilling over a hard wood fire. The wood smoke and fresh air lend an ancient element that is perfect for a gathering. Emmer is a more glutinous wheat than einkorn so it is a bit easier to handle, making it better suited to being tossed about around a fire. Each type of wheat has its own unique taste and structural properties, which makes it a lot of fun and very useful to experiment with different wheats for different applications.

Ingredients:

1 pound and 5 ounces emmer flour
2 teaspoons salt
1/2 teaspoon instant yeast
2 cups water

Things to roast, grill, and prep for filling:

Roasted goat, lamb, or beef
Red and yellow peppers and onion rings
Parsley, mint, cilantro, oregano, or thyme. (not all at the same time, though)
Most any vegetables you have on hand

Directions:

1. Mix flour with salt and yeast
2. Mix water with dry ingredients into dough with spoon
3. Allow to rise at least 30 percent in volume before using

After initial rise, limit further rising by refrigerating dough. Use for up to one week.

4. Scoop 1/3 cup of dough and pat into a round, using plenty of flour for dusting.
5. Roll out to about 6-8 inches and ⅛-1/4 inch thick
6. Use plenty of flour when patting or rolling your dough so it doesn't get stuck. You can always brush off excess flour after baking.
7. Grill for about 2 minutes per side on a hot grill.

LEMON GARLIC TAHINI SAUCE

So versatile, easy. Smash some garlic to smithereens with a garlic press, mortar and pestle, or the side of a large knife. Add salt, tahini and lemon juice. I'll put measurements below, but this is one of those sauces that is best made to suit your individual taste and application.

You can also use this as a template to create innumerable sauces. Any nut butter (sunflower, almond, peanut, etc.) can be substituted for tahini, any vinegar or acid can be substituted for lemon juice, and garlic can be replaced or added to with any alliums, like shallots, onions, scallions, or chives.

Use water to bring your sauce to the desired consistency and then check for acidity and salt. If it tastes too rich, increase acidity. If it is too tangy, add tahini.

Ingredients:

1/4 cup tahini (or other nut butter)

1-4 cloves garlic

Juice of 1-2 lemons

Water to adjust consistency

Salt and pepper to taste

The Richness of Connection

We absorb the most valuable lessons from our parents through how they live their lives. My father, a computer scientist, loved his kitchen, revered heritage grains, and always sought out foods with flavor and vitality. His father, the Head of Alcohol Studies at Rutgers, became passionate about baking after a trip through France in the early 1950s. Upon his return, he lined his home oven with fire bricks and acquired a water mister to simulate the steam injected brick ovens he saw in Europe. He boiled bagels, fermented doughs, and injected steam into the bake to facilitate a proper Maillard reaction in the crust. He was fascinated by the biochemistry and transformation in bread-making.

Ancient wheats and heirloom rice lined our cupboards when I was growing up. My father used a burr coffee mill to grind his own flours and always found the kitchen to be a primary source of pleasure and contentment. He sought food that was special, authentic, and meaningful. While traveling in Costa Rica in the 1990s, he befriended a coffee farmer and stayed with him for several nights. They wrote each other afterward, and my father bought green beans from his farm and roasted them in his kitchen for many years. I roasted coffee in my father's little old toaster oven until it finally gave out last year.

This is how food creates meaning in our lives. It is the connection we have to the history of our food source and all the people connected with it. The more we know about our food, the more meaning there is. Knowing our farmers, knowing the people who work to bring food to your table in exchange for your contribution makes our lives more gratifying and integrated.

My father was also an accomplished flutist, and initially I followed his musical inclinations more than his culinary ones, pursuing music from the time I was about 10. I was always inspired by his love of cooking , and I grew up in an experimental kitchen immersion experience. Breakfast consisted of homemade pancakes, crepes, bagels, or muffins. Lunch was leftovers punctuated by milk shakes and yogurt smoothies, and dinner could be anything from gumbo, buddha's delight, spaghetti and meatballs, to pad thai. All were made from the most authentic and best ingredients he could find, and inspired by his travels and the people and food he encountered around the world.

Dinner and baked goods were essential to a good day. He sought out international markets and local organic food co-ops, as well as up-and-coming bakeries to satisfy his craving for authentic and interesting foods. He had a small herb and vegetable garden and always stopped at roadside farm stands for the best seasonal produce. He brought home organic yogurt from a small dairy in New Hampshire and explained to me that "this was the good stuff." My friends liked to stay for dinner, though it was sometimes an unusual experience for them; most of them had grown up on frozen factory-made dinners and school cafeteria lunch. They could taste something different. They'd say, "Your dad cooks some strange food, but it's good!"

In the fall of 2000, when I was just shy of twenty years old, I was down in my basement music studio at my mother's, practicing percussion, when I was called by my mother to pick up the phone. It was my dad. (My parents had separated years earlier.) I couldn't call him back? It was extremely unusual for my father to call me like that, and I was immediately concerned. It was not unfounded. He had been experiencing stomach pains for several months and had been to the doctor again. The news was not good. He had been diagnosed with pancreatic cancer and would most likely lose the battle to it in the next six months.

My world was rocked. My father was my best friend. At 53, he was recently remarried, enjoying his life more than ever, and could not believe the news. Once pancreatic cancer is detectable, it's almost always too late. My step mother, Nancy, sister Jessica, and I took care of my father throughout his illness, and he passed away the following May. I was devastated.

Eventually, cooking and baking became my way of staying connected with my father and still is to this day. His joy and passion and the myriad of memories I have from childhood are a constant source of love, support and inspiration. I can still see him so vividly admiring in wonderment about the magic of muffins and the simple seeds that yielded so much pleasure and seemingly endless interest.

PIZZA

THE PERFECT CANVAS FOR TRADITIONS OLD AND NEW

Bread and cheese with vegetables and herbs. Crustaceans and clams, grandma style, original Neapolitan, smoked salmon with dill, Detroit, chicken bacon Ranch, steak burrito..the list goes on and on. No pizza stone has been left unturned at this point (pun intended!). As it turns out, there are very few things that you can put between hot bread and cheese that won't work. Even cheeseless salad pizza can be fantastically delicious!

This is essentially the same as the french bread recipe, except that it can be used for an hour or two after mixing and for up to 10 days in the fridge. I enjoy it most at about 24 hours. If you are new to making pizza, use baking trays and make smaller sizes. As you get more comfortable handling the dough, you can go bigger.

Traditional Neapolitan style dough is made strictly with water, flour, salt, and yeast while variations around the world often add small amounts of sugar and oil. I suggest starting from a traditional dough and then adding in small amounts of sugar or oil to see if you like the adjustment. I personally prefer the traditional style without these additions.

Sugar and oil will have two main effects. It will soften the dough and lower the browning temperature. The more sugar you add, the lower your oven temperature will need to be. If you are working with whole flours, the shortening effect of oil and sugar also becomes less desirable. Since whole wheat doughs are more flavorful, these doughs really don't need "more". Keep it simple and discover the greatest pizzas of your life! It's all about the quality of your ingredients and how you prepare them for the pizza.

The topping schemes are limitless, and whether you choose classic topping arrangements or if you are going off the beaten track, you can still satisfy your need for a trip to culinary greatness!

Ingredients:

1 pound 5 ounces Redeemer flour

2 teaspoons salt

1/2 teaspoon instant yeast

2 cups water

Are you noticing a trend here? This particular ratio generally hits the sweet spot where the ideal balance of ingredients yields an incredibly versatile dough. This is a perfect starting place to explore the multitude of variations possible, but start here first. Once you have become familiar with this dough and how it behaves in different circumstances with a variety of wheats, start to explore one variable at a time. Make small adjustments and be prepared - changing even one variable may create a complex interaction. Pay very close attention and prepare to be delighted and confounded… it's part of the adventure!

Directions:

1. Mix your dry ingredients together in a mixing bowl.
2. Add water at a seasonally appropriate temperature (100-110 degrees in the winter, 80 degrees in spring and fall, and around 60 degrees in the summer. The point is to get your dough to about 78 degrees after mixing).
3. Mix thoroughly with a spoon or fork.
4. Allow to rise 30-50 percent before using or place in the refrigerator for use anytime in the next 3 days. You can also freeze for up to 10 days.
5. Portion and prepare all your toppings. You never want to roll out your dough before getting your toppings perfectly prepped and at the ready. Once your dough is rolled, it needs to be topped immediately and go right into the oven so it doesn't get stuck.
6. Preheat your oven to 450 degrees.
7. Portion out about 12 ounces of dough for a large thin crust or adjust according to the desired size and thickness you want your pizzas to be.
8. Use plenty of flour to dust your dough, work surface, and your peel or baking tray. Don't skimp here! If you use too much, you can easily dust it off afterward. If you use too little, it could get stuck somewhere along the line and possibly ruin your pizza.
9. Use a rolling pin to roll out to the desired length and thickness (this is the pin I highly recommend).
10. Top your pizza and load into the oven until nicely browned on the top and bottom, about 20-25 minutes.

Grilled Pizza with spinach, ricotta,
pickled and caramelized onions, steak and Stilton

GRILLED PIZZA

Grilled pizza was popularized in the 1980's at Al Forno in Providence RI. The touch of smoky grilled bread underneath topping that are already cooked or don't need cooking is a special treat. The pizza dough is grilled for 2-4 minutes on one side and then flipped.

While the pizza dough finishes cooking on the second side toppings are added and a flash under the broiler can provide a little extra cheese melt if desired. The steak, black bean, and duck pizza are all grilled. Some types of pizza call for topping that either shouldn't be cooked aren't as good cooked twice. Grilled pizza is the perfect solution!

GRILLED PIZZA WITH BLACK BEANS, GRILLED CHICKEN, AVOCADO, SUMMER SQUASH AND FETA

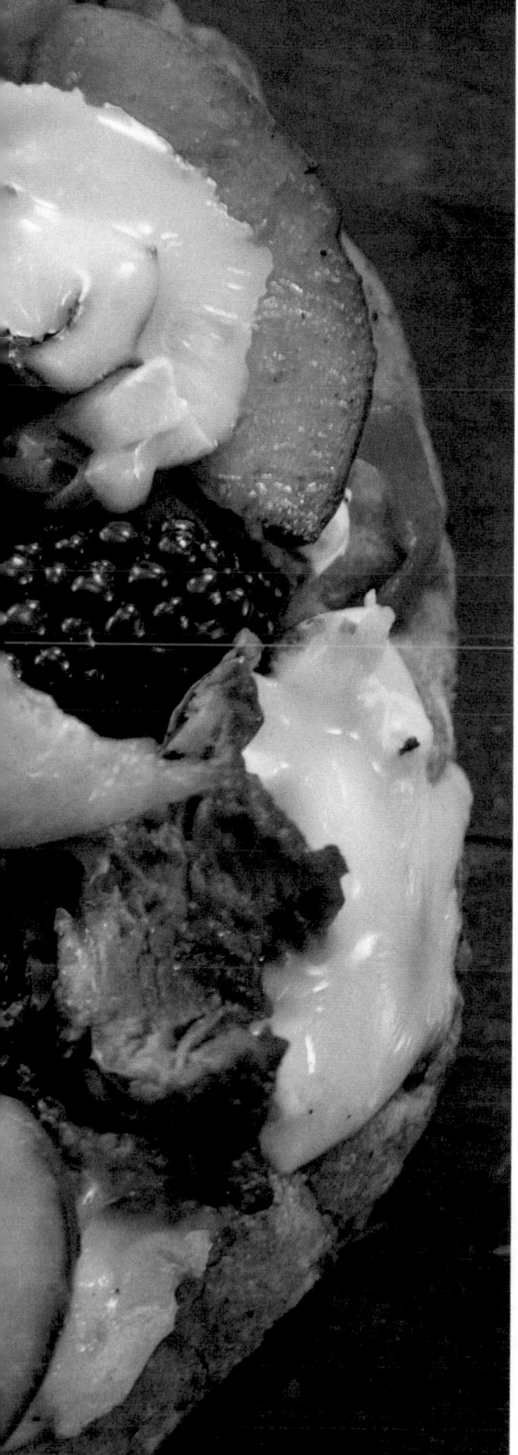

Duck Pizza

with Brie and Seasonal Fruits

I first made a duck pizza many years ago when figuring out what to do with leftover duck from a holiday roast. Usually I would use the leg to make duck confit (slow cooked submerged in duck fat) and use the fall-off-the-bone confit. Here I didn't have time for that but still wanted to revisit this old favorite with the bursting fresh flavors of summer and an unctuous triple cream brie. Underscored by the peppery arugula, this was a real treat, although if I were to make it again I would stick to one or two fruits instead of all three. I also used the rest of the pickled onions from the steak pizza to add a touch of zing to balance all the rich and sweet flavors. I grilled the pizza crust and then topped it with the arugula, cooked duck breast, lightly sauteed peaches, blackberries, cherries, and then the brie. I flashed it under the broiler to melt the cheese a touch without cooking the duck breast any further.

PIZZA MOUSAKKA

The Greek national dish (and an old favorite of mine) is the lamb and eggplant casserole moussaka. Almost any dish you can think of can be adapted for a pizza version. Here I cooked the onions, garlic, summer squash and tomatoes together while the eggplant is roasted whole. I also made a bechamel sauce and seasoned and spice the ground lamb. After rolling out the dough, I topped it first with the tomato sauce, oregano, and mint, then the roasted eggplant, ground lamb, bechamel, and finally topped it off with some aged gouda. This is certainly not the traditional moussaka, but all traditions start as a creative idea.

Always make sure your sauces are not too moist or your pizza will get soggy. Likewise, avoid putting raw vegetables that will release lots of moisture while cooking like raw tomato. Best to cook them ahead and release excess moisture before the pizza bakes. I used tomato paste to thicken the sauce to the right moisture level.

Ingredients:

1. 1 large eggplant (roasted whole until thoroughly soft)
2. 1/3 pound ground lamb (seasoned with salt, pepper, cumin, and coriander)
3. 1/2 onion
4. 3 cloves garlic
5. 1 small summer squash
6. 1 tomato
7. About 2 ounces tomato paste (enough to thicken sauce)
8. 2 tablespoons flour and oil for the bechamel plus 1 cup milk or water
9. Mint and oregano
10. 4-6 ounces of cheese...there are many cheeses that could work well here. Take a break from mozzarella and try something different. I think gouda would be particularly good here but the choices are endless. Goats cheese, pecorino, or gruyere would also be excellent.

Deep Dish Loaded Potato

I had my first deep dish pizza in central Connecticut in the mid 1990s while traveling with my father. It was the first time I had been to a pizza restaurant that served pizza other than New York style. They had a deep dish red potato and ricotta pizza that blew us away and brought us back again and again. This pizza is a spin between the classic loaded baked potato and that ricotta pie we had all those years ago. I made the crust out of einkorn so it would be a little more pastry-like and used a 9 inch cast iron pan as the vehicle, though you could use almost any baking dish like a pie pan or casserole dish.

Ingredients:

Dough recipe from page 49 made with einkorn flour
3 large red or yukon potatoes
1.5-2 cups whole milk ricotta
1 head of broccoli
2-4 strips of thick-cut bacon
1 cup low moisture mozzarella, cheddar, or any favorite cheese

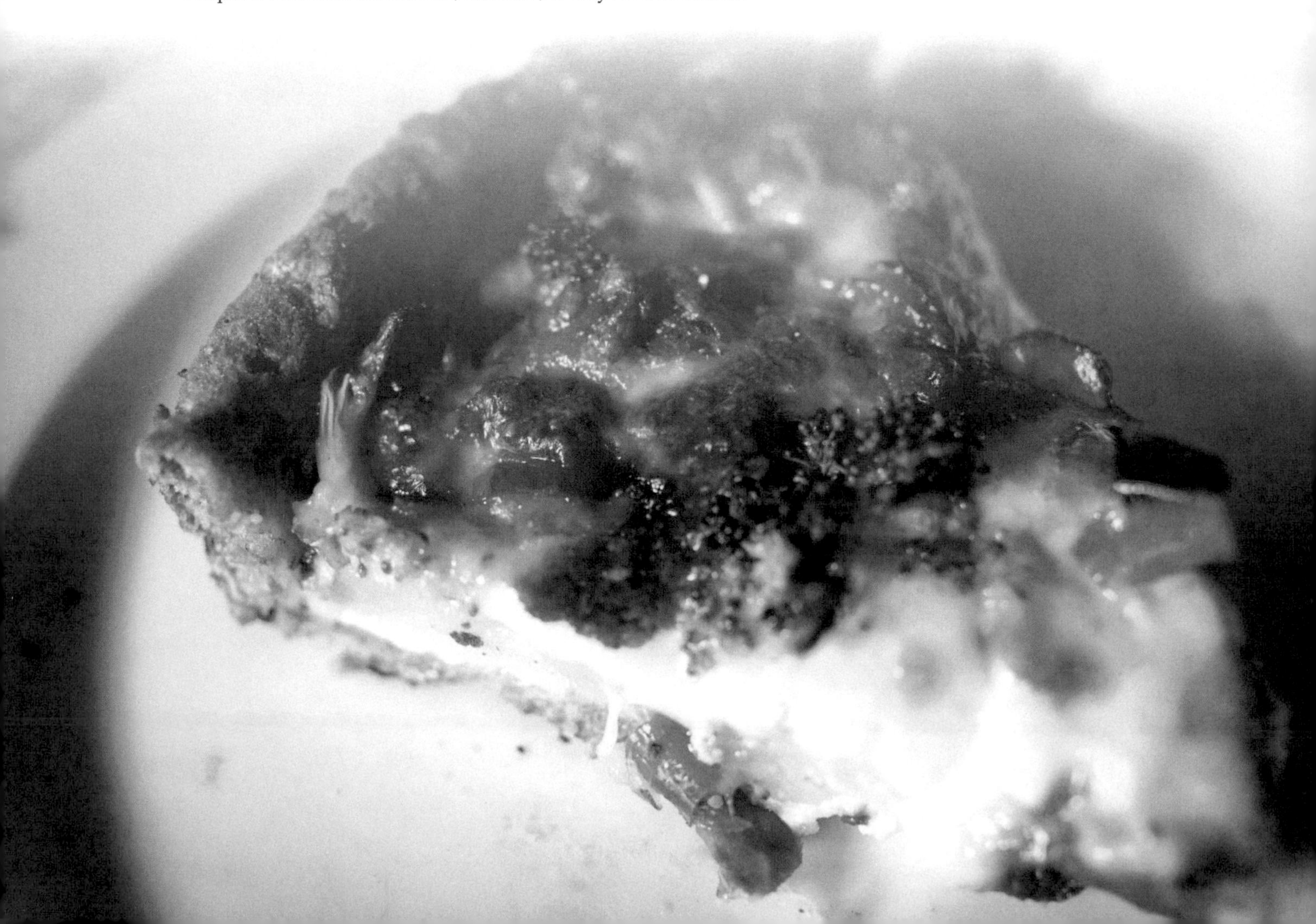

Directions:

1. Use the same formula for the dough from p.49, substituting einkorn flour.
2. Bake potatoes and prep the raw broccoli.
3. Cook bacon 80% of the way and chop roughly. Grate cheese and grease pan.
4. Roll out the dough and press into your pan, making the edges a little thicker than the bottom.
5. Cover the bottom of the pie generously with ricotta (at least 1/4 inch).
6. Slice the potatoes 1/4-1/3 inch thick and layer on top of the ricotta.
7. Cover with grated mozzarella or cheddar (or any favorite cheese).
8. Top with bacon and broccoli and a touch more cheese and bake at 400 degrees for about 40 minutes.

WHOLE WHEAT LAVASH

THIN WHEAT FLATBREADS

YELLOW EYE FALAFEL AND HUMMUS, BHABAGHANOUSH AND CUCUMBER TOMOATO SALAD

This preparation is very similar to pita, except the dough is rolled and stretched to the thinnest possible sheet and baked in less than two minutes on a very hot pan, griddle, or in a tandoor oven. The thinner it is and the longer it bakes the more quickly it will become a cracker both on and off the griddle. The biggest challenge is getting the thin lavash dough from your rolling station to the griddle without it folding or tearing too much. While it's traditional to use a pillow to do the final stretching and to flip the lavash into place, a simple method you can use is to do your final stretching of the dough on a silicone mat or a piece of parchment paper and use that to flip it onto the griddle or into your pan (a 10-14 inch pan of any sort will do). You'll want to use plenty of flour on both sides as you roll it out and you may have to let the dough rest once or twice for a minute or two to allow the dough to relax while it is getting stretched to its limits. Don't force it. Roll it a little and then do another task and repeat until the dough is thin and fairly even, dusting and flipping frequently. You'll notice a tendency for the dough to get overly thin in the middle and to stay to thicker around the edges. As you roll, pay extra attention to rolling the outer edges. When you do your final stretch of the dough, focus on thinning out the edges, not the middle.

Yellow Eye Hummus

Soak your beans overnight or in hot water for 1-2 hours and then cook until soft. Put all ingredients in your food processor and process until completely smooth. Put in serving bowl and sprinkle with chili, thyme, sumac olive oil and turmeric for an extra touch
.

1 pound yellow eye beans
1/4 cup tahini
1/8 cup garlic cloves
2 tablespoons olive oil
Juice of one medium lemon
1/8 teaspoon turmeric
1/8 teaspoon cumin
2 teaspoons salt
1/2 teaspoon black pepper

Falafel

Soak yellow eye beans overnight. Place all ingredients into a food processor and process until a sand-like texture that will hold shape when you press into a shape for frying.

1 pound yellow eye beans
Juice of one medium lemon
3-4 cloves of garlic
1/8 cup chopped parsley
1/4 teaspoon cumin
1/8 teaspoon coriander
2 teaspoons salt
1/8 teaspoon black pepper
1 tablespoon sesame seeds
1 tablespoon Aleppo pepper or other chili flakes/powder

Lavash Bread

Ingredients:

1lb 5.5oz Redeemer wheat flour

2 cups water

2 teaspoons salt

1 teaspoon instant yeast or 1/4 cup sourdough starter

Directions:

1. Mix your dry ingredients together.
2. Combine with water until thoroughly mixed.
3. Allow the dough to ferment for at least 45 minutes. Use very warm water for a quick result. You can also use cool water and place in the refrigerator to use later or the following day.
4. Using your 1/4 cup measure, scoop out a piece of dough and gently massage into a disc shape (use 1/3 cup scoop for larger lavash).
5. Using lots of dusting flour on both sides, begin to roll the disc into a thinner and thinner round, keeping it well-coated in flour.
6. Once the dough is about 3 millimeters thick, move it onto the silicone mat or parchment paper. Do your final rolling or stretching and place on your griddle or into the oven.
7. Lavash can be cooked anywhere from as little as 1 minute to as long as several minutes - it really depends on the thickness of your dough and the temperature of your oven.

Play around and have fun! There is no one right way to do anything and the more you practice the better you'll get.

Bhabaghanoush

Cube and steam one large eggplant. Add 1/3 cup tahini and the juice and zest of one lemon, 1 table-spoon of minced or pressed garlic, salt and pepper to taste and enough water to achieve the desired consistency. Mash with a potato masher or toss in the blender/food processor and you've arrived! It only takes 15 minutes.

Cucumber Tomato Salad

Simple, fresh, juicy, and vibrant. Variations on this quintessential salad abound, so find the best tomatoes and cukes you can get your hands on and mix with lemon juice and parsley and then personalize to your heart's content! Salt and pep-per to taste and it's ready. This will keep for up to a week in your refrigerator, but is best in the first couple days

Pickled Vegetables

Most vegetables make great quick pickles. Some of my favorites are celeriac, carrots, onions, bell pep-pers, and cauliflower, but almost any vegetables can be used... experiment and find your favorite! To keep it simple, place your chopped veggies in a mason jar packed tight. Cover with about 1/3 of the jar with your preferred vinegar and the rest water. Add a teaspoon of salt spices and herbs and even a dash of something sweet if it calls to you.

EGGPLANT REVELATIONS...

I love eggplant. I grew up eating eggplant parmesan grinders and never lost the taste for it, craving it every season by the time August hits without fail each year. However, as I first began to prepare it myself I discovered mostly complicated, unsuccessful ways suggested to prepare it in almost every cookbook I owned and online.

Salting and rinsing and sauteing!? If you have an entire hour to work on your eggplant and want a lot of oil soaked up by the eggplant preparation, go for it.

My two favorite ways take almost zero effort and yield perfectly cooked eggplant every time, which you can use to make moussaka, baba ganoush, eggplant parmesan, miso glazed, the list goes on and on.

Simplest: Simply poke some holes in a whole eggplant and roast at 350 for about 40-60 minutes until cooked through and totally soft.

Quickest: Cube eggplant and place in a small pot with a lid and 1/4 inch of water in the bottom of the pan. Steam until tender, about ten minutes.

Two more quick tips for cooking eggplant: first, do not remove the skin. It is the best part and chock full of nutrients! The skin of purple eggplants contains its most valuable nutrient, a powerful antioxidant called nasunin, a type of flavonoid called anthocyanins present in many fruits and vegetables with red, blue and purple hues (berries, beets and red cabbage, to name a few). Also, the bitterness you may taste comes from the oil burning in the pan, not the eggplant. Eggplant is not bitter at all.

ANCIENT EINKORN AND EMMER MATZA

AND MY GREAT GRANDMOTHER RIFKA'S MATZA BALL SOUP

That night, they are to eat the meat, roasted in the fire; they are to eat it with matzo and maror.
– Exodus 12:8

While I am not religious per se, making matzah is certainly a spiritual act for me.The fact that these types of breads have been prepared for thousands of years makes it an act that connects us to so many generations of our ancestors in such a profound way. You don't even need salt to make it - just flour and water.

Any type of wheat you use will work, but each will bring its own unique flavor and texture. It is a great way to really become acquainted with the properties of different wheats, as there is nothing to complicate the matter. Once the water is baked out, all you have left is the toasted wheat. While typically matza is mostly eaten at Passover, matzo ball soup is always a welcome treat and provides its own sense of connection and place in our lives, kind of like a warm hug from your grandma.

Matza can be made with any type of wheat, barley, rye, and oats, although wheat is most common. The matza from biblical times would have been made mostly from wheat and barley. Bread was used as both a plate and as an eating utensil and likely would have been served soft when freshly baked.

Emmer makes both a darker colored flour and resulting matza (above Einkorn on left and emmer on right). Also, the emmer was steamed during the baking and the einkorn was not, giving the emmer matza a sheen while the einkorn ones have a more flour-dusted look without the steam during the bake.

Ingredients:

14 ounces flour
1 cup water

Directions:

1. Preheat your oven to 450 degrees.
2. Mix your dough and allow to rest for 5-10 minutes.
3. Portion your dough into five or six rounds. I like to use a 1/3 cup scoop to portion nice rounds easily.
4. Prepare several sheet pans with parchment paper or silicone baking mats. If you don't have these, you can just dust your sheet pans heavily with flour (that's what we did for this shoot).
5. Take your round dough portions and roll them into rounds, using plenty of flour for dusting both sides so they don't stick. Ancient wheats make a stickier dough than modern wheat, so use extra flour in that case.
6. Before they are all the way rolled out and can still be moved, place them on your parchment or silicone lined baking trays.
7. Do any final rolling to get them even and thin and load into the oven.
8. Bake until crisp and nicely browned.

MATZA BALL SOUP

To make matza ball soup from matza, you have to grind your matza into meal or flour. I use my food processor to grind it coarsely and then run it through my grain mill to make flour out of it. It's a bit of work, but I would not have included it in this book if it didn't make something truly special. These matza balls are as delicious and satisfying as a perfect meatball and truly take chicken soup to a higher level

Be sure not to overbake your matza, which could cause your matza balls to taste burnt and have a dense texture.

Ingredients:

1. 3/4 cup matza meal

2. 3 eggs

3. 6 tablespoons smaltz (chicken fat), or butter or vegetable oil as substitutes

4. 1/6 cup chicken stock or water

5. 1 1/2 tablespoons chopped parsley (use half chopped stems, they add texture and moisture)

6. 1 teaspoon salt

7. 1/4 teaspoon black pepper

8. 1/4 teaspoon ground nutmeg (microplaning whole nutmeg is best)

9. 1/6 cup finely diced onion

Directions:

1. Combine all ingredients in a large mixing bowl and mix together.
2. Place mixture in the refrigerator and allow to chill for 1-3 hours.
3. Scoop golf ball sized pieces and roll between hands to round.
4. Place balls into gently simmering chicken stock that has been seasoned.
5. Cook until desired tenderness has been reached, about 30 to 60 minutes.
7. Once the matza balls are cooked to your liking, serve immediately or freeze any extra for later use.

SMOKED CHILI AND GARLIC NAAN

WITH LAMB BIRYANI AND CUCUMBER RAITA

Naan Bread is very similar to pita bread except that is enriched with a small amount of yogurt, fat, and sugar. Here I am adding chili and garlic to spice it up, but of course you can omit these if you like your naan mild. This dough can be ready to use in as little as 30 minutes or instantly, in a pinch (if you use baking powder/soda). It can also last in your fridge for several days for daily naan making. Traditionally baked in a tandoori oven, these can be easily baked in pan or on a griddle.

Ingredients:

1 pound 5oz sifted Redeemer flour
2 teaspoons fine sea salt
1/2 to 2 teaspoons instant yeast
1 cup water
4 ounces yoghurt
1 teaspoon honey
2 teaspoon butter or ghee
1 tablespoon smoked green chili sauce (Hosta Hill is the best)

Directions:

1. First you need to decide how much yeast to use. This will depend on when you want your dough to be ready to use. If you need it in 30 minutes, use the full 2 teaspoons and make sure the dough is at least 80-90 degrees. If you are making it the day before, use 1/2 teaspoon instant yeast.
2. Mix dry ingredients together and then mix wet ingredients together.
3. The dough should rise in volume at least 30% before using. A 50%-100% increase is better.

4. Preheat a griddle or pan until just starting to smoke slightly (about 350-400 degrees surface temperature), or preheat your oven to 500 degrees.
5. Bake or griddle until dark spots have formed on one side.
6. Slather in turmeric, ghee, or butter, scoop up some raita and lamb biryani, and prepare to enter heaven!

Lamb Biryani

1/2 pound to 1 pound cubed leg of lamb
1 whole eggplant, cubed
4-6 cups spinach
4-6 crushed garlic cloves
1/2 onion
1/cup tomato puree
2 teaspoons masala or other preferred Indian spice mix.
1/4 cup cubed paneer
1 tablespoon smoked green chili sauce
1/2 cup cashews
1/4 cup golden raisins
1/4 cup dried apricots
Salt to taste

Directions:

1. In a cooking pot, add onion, garlic, tomato puree, and spice blend and simmer until tender (about 10 minutes).
2. Add eggplant, cashews, raisins, and apricots and cook 5-10 minutes
3. Stir in the spinach, lamb and paneer and turn off the heat to allow a gentle finish to the cooking. your meat should be cubed not larger than 1 inch so it will be cooked through. Be careful not to over cook the lamb!
4. Cook one cup of rice and stir together or serve separately. I am partial to Erik's rice but you can use the traditional basmati

Cucumber Raita

Ingredients:

4oz yogurt
1/4 cup diced red onion
1/4 cup diced cucumber
Spice blend to taste
Salt to taste
Stir together and enjoy!

WHEAT TORTILLAS
BURRITOS AND QUESADILLAS

Burritos and quesadillas are another way an entire section of a cuisine has been organized around flatbreads. They are so versatile, delicious, and practical, there is no way not to enjoy them! Stuffed with beans, cheese, vegetables, and meat, or flattened out for extra crispiness with beans omitted, these are a culinary classic heralding from northern Mexico and popularized throughout the world. While I make these both whole wheat and with sifted flour, I definitely recommend starting with a sifted flour, as these must be rolled out very thin. I recommend the same technique used on the lavash for rolling and flipping your tortillas. Any bean or legume can be used, but I prefer Jacob's Cattle for a perfect "refried bean"(in this case, the refried just refers to the double cooking; I use no oil when I prepare beans).

You can add rice to your burritos as well, but this is not the original north Mexican style. Personally, I prefer the original style. Chorizo and egg or steak with spinach combined with the beans, melted cheese, poblanos, summer squash, and onions, some raw red onion, and sour cream is an explosion of deliciousness. Customize it to suit your taste with whatever is seasonally available and it is hard to go wrong.

Ingredients:

1lb 6oz sifted Redeemer wheat
1/2 teaspoon baking powder
1/2 teaspoon baking soda
1 1/2 teaspoon salt
2 cups water
2 tablespoons lard (or substitute butter or vegetable oil)

Directions:

1. Mix together dry ingredients.
2. Mix water and oil with dry ingredients until a slightly stiff dough forms.
3. Leave dough to relax for 30 minutes.

4. Prepare fillings. I like sauteed onions and poblanos but almost any vegetable combo will work. Summer squash, bell peppers, and spinach are all very good as well. Spices like cumin and coriander are very complimentary.
5. Melt your cheese into the beans and saute any protein of choice.
6. Here I also steamed spinach with garlic and a dash of salt.
7. Take 1/4 to 1/3 cup of dough and roll into a very thin round on a silpat with plenty of flour to eliminate sticking. You may need to roll the tortilla with a rest in the middle. Make sure to focus on rolling the edges out, as they tend to be thicker than the middle.
8. Preheat a 12 inch pan or griddle to medium-high heat and flip tortilla onto the dry pan.
9. Flip after 2 minutes and finish for 1 minute on the second side.
10. Roll up your favorite fillings and enjoy!

To make quesadillas, follow the same tortilla making process as the burrito, but be prepared to use half as much filling and pan fry on both sides to finish and melt the cheese. Here I omitted the beans and switched the protein to shrimp. Be creative!

SPRING PANCAKES

HOISIN SAUCE, PEKING DUCK AND MOO SHU PORK

Spring pancakes originated from the northern regions of China, dating back to at least 1,500 years ago. Traditionally they would be eaten on the Lichun to celebrate the beginning of spring. These chewy little wrappers are also used to make "spring rolls' when filled and deep fried. Hoisin or black bean sauce is the essential condiment here. Made with fermented soybeans known as black beans, sugar (or honey), rice wine vinegar, sesame paste, chili, garlic, and rice wine. Hoisin is the sweeter, smoother version while black bean sauce is a little textured and less sweet. I like to make the black bean sauce style and sweeten with a little honey for hoisin if I need to. Armed with pancakes and hoisin, there are endless incredible meals. Preparing lots of little fillings and letting everyone build their own perfect wrap is a fun way to go. If you don't have the Chinese black beans on hand, Japanese miso make an excellent substitute. That said, make sure you pick up some salted black beans at your local Chinese market for an incredible flavor that is essential to the Chinese cuisine and flavors.

Hoisin Sauce

Ingredients:

1/2 cup salted black beans
1/3 cup honey
1/4 cup rice wine vinegar
2 tablespoons sesame paste (tahini)
1 tablespoon rice wine
2 teaspoons grated garlic and ginger
1 teaspoon salt
1/8 teaspoon 5 spice powder

Directions:

1. For the "old style," combine ingredients and mash together.
2. For the "hoisin" style, increase the honey to 1/2 cup and blend until smooth in a food processor, blender, or mortar and pestle.
3. Enjoy as a dipping sauce, add to stir fry, or marinate and glaze meat with this epic sauce. It will also keep indefinitely in your refrigerator.

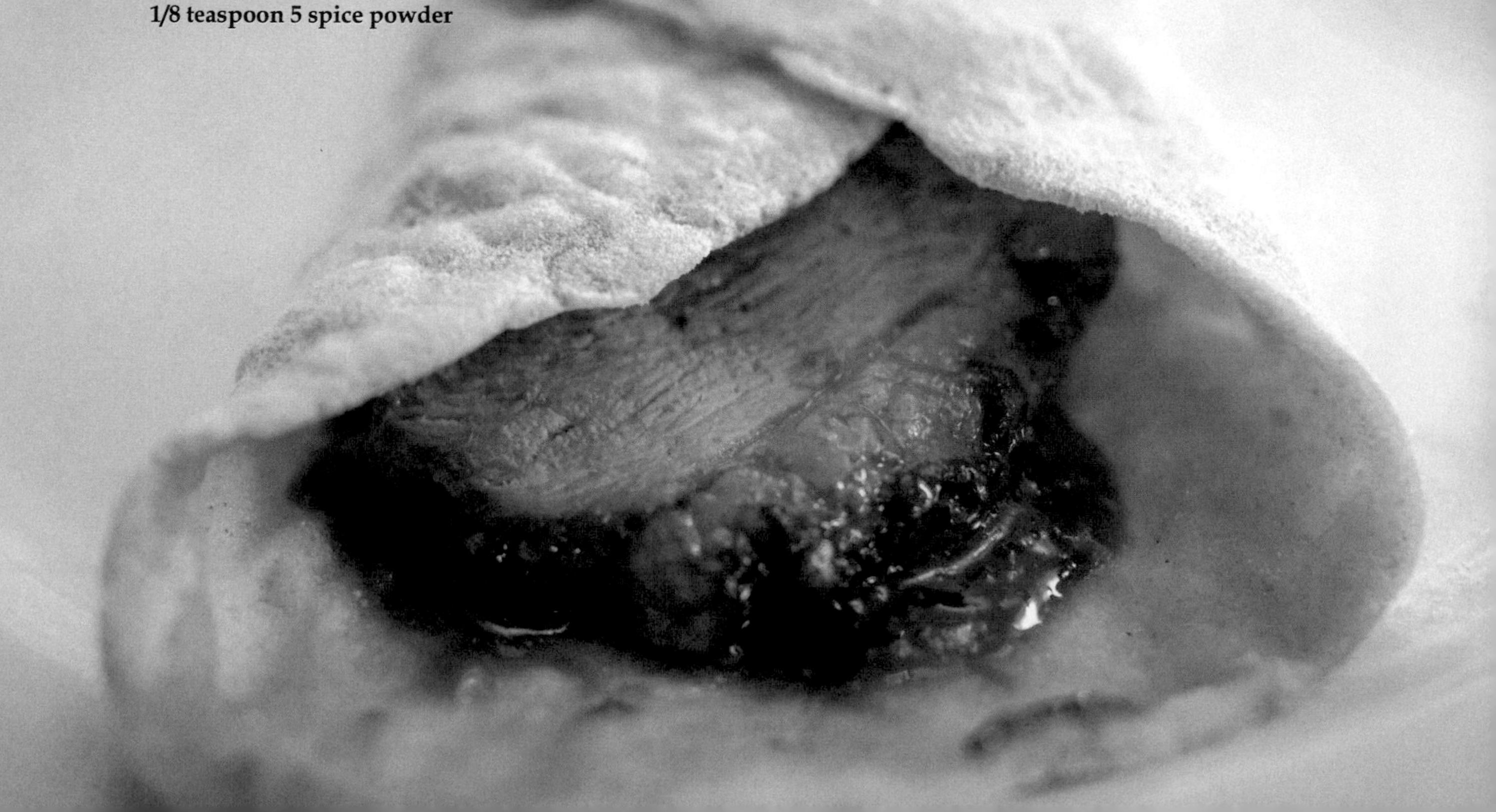

Spring Pancakes

Ingredients:

1. 2 cups sifted Redeemer flour

2. 1 teaspoon fine sea salt

3. 1 tablespoon sesame oil

4. 1 cup boiling water

Directions:

1. Combine dry ingredients and mix thoroughly.
2. Heat water and add sesame oil to water.
3. Combine wet and dry ingredients and mix into a soft dough.
4. Let dough rest for 30 minutes.
5. Scoop dough into 1 oz portions (heaping tablespoon).
6. Dust with flour, flatten, and roll into 4 inch rounds.
7. Brush sesame oil almost to the edge of one round, then place a second round on top.
8. Roll the two pieces together until 1/8 inch thick and about 7-8 inches around.
9. Heat pan to medium high heat.
10. In dry pan, cook pancakes for about 2 minutes per side or until brown dots appear.

11. Allow to cool and then peel apart.
12. Spread with hoisin sauce and wrap up your favorite fillings.

Moo Shu Pork

While this dish originates from the Shandong province like the pancakes, it has changed in Chinese American cuisine to adapt to available ingredients. The Chinese version is made with pork, egg, bamboo shoots, day lily, and wood ear mushrooms, and the same seasoning of soy sauce, rice wine, sesame oil, garlic, and ginger; the Chinese American version has replaced the cucumber and day lilies with cabbage and carrots. Also Chinese Moo Shu pork is not served with spring pancakes as we do in America.

I'd like to point out that these are both completely legitimate traditions. Sometimes there is a tendency to call older traditions "authentic" and newer or adaptive traditions "not authentic". While this serves a purpose to help maintain useful "proven trends" versus a new idea or worse an attempt to take advantage of a tradition to trick people into paying for low quality goods or services. The chinese American food traditions are now over 150 years old with the first restaurant hailing from the 1850's in Sanfransico. These are genuine traditions already well set into their cultural tracks and while they are different than cuisine in China they are very much authentic Chinese American cuisine.

Ingredients:

1/2 pound thinly sliced pork loin or tenderloin
3 eggs beaten
3/4 cup rehydrated wood ear mushrooms sliced thin (black trumpet or morel make good substitutions).
1 cup chopped daylilies or bamboo shoots
3/4 cup summer squash or cucumber in 1/4 inch half rounds
1 cup finely shredded green cabbage
1/2 cup julienned or grated carrots
2 scallions
5 oz of grated ginger
1 tablespoon sesame oil
2 tablespoons soy sauce
1 tablespoon cooking rice wine

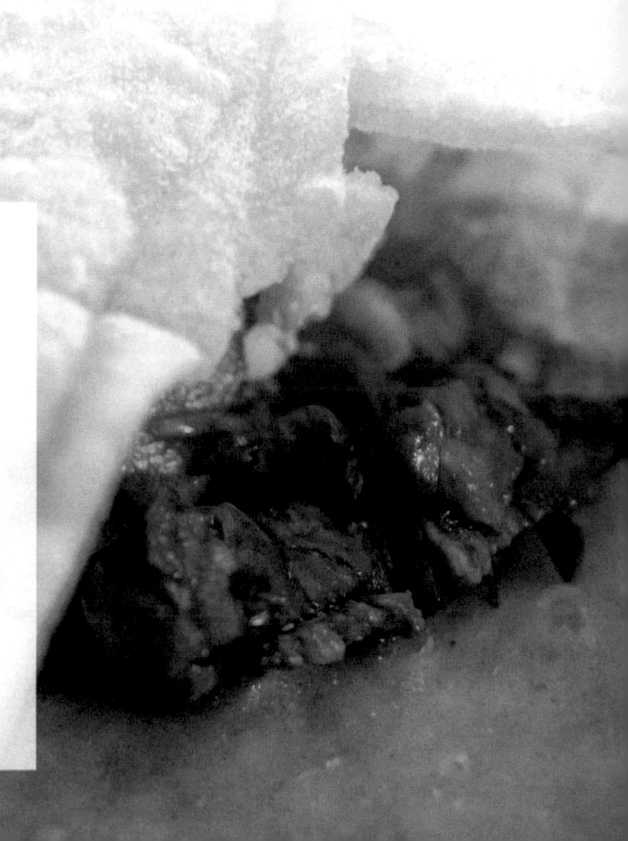

Directions:

1. This is a simply a stir fry. Prep all your ingredients ahead of time, as it only need to cook for a few minutes.
2. I prefer to cook my eggs separately and set aside.
3. Start with the carrots, then add the mushrooms, cabbage, and squash.
4. Add the soy sauce and cooking wine, finishing with the scallions and pork so as not to overcook. Take off the heat as these go in. Allow several minutes for the carry over cooking to finish the pork. Taste for seasoning; you can add a little hoisin if you want to bump up the flavor quickly.

PEKING DUCK

This incredible glazed roast duck is something for a real celebration. While not difficult to make, it does need to hang to dry for about 24 hours in order to end up with crispy skin. You can skip the drying if you're not attached to the crispy skin and makes this in an afternoon, or glaze a duck breast if you want to make a simple and smaller version.

For the full restaurant style version, you'll need to hang your duck overnight in your refrigerator. The following day, make the sweet and sour glaze and glaze the inside and outside of the duck, coating thoroughly for about 5 minutes. Hang the duck again until the glaze has dried (about 4 hours). Then place the duck on a vertical chicken/duck roaster and roast at 300 degrees until the thickest part of the thigh near the bone (but not on) reaches 175 degrees. If you skip the dry hanging and don't bother with a vertical roaster, it will still be very delicious, but not crispy. Also if you very carefully slide your hand in between the skin and the body to separate the two, it will be even crispier.

If you're cooking for one or two and have limited time, you can use duck breast too. Dry the duck breast in your fridge after patting dry with a paper towel. Score the skin in a checkered pattern and pan fry skin side down until crispy, flip the breast over and finish in the oven until the internal temperature is 130 degrees. This will carry over to about 130-135 degrees for a perfect medium rare.

Peking Duck Glaze

Ingredients:

3 cups water
2 scallions
1/6 cup honey
2 slices of ginger
1 tablespoon plus 2 teaspoons cornstarch
1 tablespoon rice vinegar

From the day we moved to Main Street, one of our primary objectives has been to create a genuine farm-to-table operation. We were tired of seeing places advertise local foods and then find only a single token local product, if that. We would have local ingredients "whenever available" (the token way to say we want to profit from the idea but not deliver it) and in the Pioneer Valley, they're almost always available. All of our meats, cheeses, and dairy were produced locally. More than 90 percent of our vegetables were grown locally, but interestingly, grain was didn't really fit easily into this picture.

When we started in 2005, certified organic flour from Champlain Valley Milling, NY or Lindley Mills, NC (the mill company that makes King Arthur organic flours, whose conventional flours are produced by ConAgra) was about 15 cents a pound. By 2007, it was 25 cents a pound. Overnight in February 2008, it went to more than 90 cents a pound. Suddenly, local grains were no longer many times the price of their commodity counterparts, but nearly the same; at the time, it cost between 75 cents and $1.50 a pound to produce small-scale organic grains for wholesale. This shift was monumental for our business, and made it economically possible to build more infrastructure around supplying and distributing local grains to the community.

Facing these massive changes, I asked myself, "Where is the opportunity? How could we turn these instabilities and disruptions into positive movement for the future?" There were a few farms growing a small amount of wheat, but there wasn't a lot going on in our immediate area. I asked a farm to grow wheat for us, but when I tried to get seed for them I learned that wheat seed was scarce. There were only one or two modern varieties available on the market, and it wasn't the type of wheat we wanted to grow. We wanted the genuine article, not something dreamed up in a laboratory or corporate boardroom. Real heritage wheat was all that would do. But where had all of our heritage wheats gone? I will also note that some modern varieties of wheat are very good - we've come to enjoy a variety called Redeemer very much. It is not genetically modified and is grown organically by the White Family in Hardwick and has fantastic flavor and baking qualities. It is a small but important part of our share each year.

There are hundreds of thousands of varieties and many different species of wheat. As an avid grower of heirloom tomatoes, salad greens, and field squash, I wanted the heirloom equivalents for wheat. They were not available through seed catalogs, but it turns out that the USDA National Small Grains Collection holds tens of thousands of wheat seed germplasms as well as genetic tissues for most other small grains. I began the process of wheat trialling to find "landrace" wheats that would grow well in the soil and climate of the Pioneer Valley. The USDA sent me many small packets of about 30 seeds each, and I began to grow many tiny patches of wheat and other grains to find what would work best in our soils and climate.

Over the next year, while I immersed myself in growing wheat cultivars, perfecting agricultural production techniques, and conducting trials, I began to realize that what was really important was not just wheat or bakeries. It was all of the heritage grains that we've lost to modern industrial and economic forces that prevail when production is hidden and costs are externalized. The community of local food eaters, foodies, and sustainable food initiatives needed access to all of our heritage grains, and the creation of a Community Supported Agriculture program based around grains and beans struck me as essential and thrilling. Thus, the Pioneer Valley Heritage Grain CSA was born. Some of my closest advisers thought I was crazy, but I knew that I was on to something.

Over the next year, while I immersed myself in growing wheat cultivars, perfecting agricultural production techniques, and conducting trials, I began to realize that what was really important was not just wheat or bakeries. It was all of the heritage grains that we've lost to modern industrial and economic forces that prevail when production is hidden and costs are externalized. The community of local food eaters, foodies, and sustainable food initiatives needed access to all of our heritage grains, and the creation of a Community Supported Agriculture program based around grains and beans struck me as essential and thrilling. Thus, the Pioneer Valley Heritage Grain CSA was born. Some of my closest advisers thought I was crazy, but I knew that I was on to something.

When you know who grows your food, and they know the people they're growing it forIt brings farm more meaning and value to the system. More meaningful personal relationships develop. Farmers get higher prices per pound while at the same time reducing waste. Consumers have access to affordable foods that are otherwise unavailable, hard to get, or very expensive. My role has been to demonstrate how to easily, healthfully, and joyfully you can integrate these ideas and foods into your kitchen. It's my labor of love.

As the idea for the grain CSA took root, I was filled with hope and determination. In the economic chaos, I believed my response made fundamental sense. In the first year, my wheat and other small grain and dry bean trials had been very successful. Yields and quality were good on numerous varieties and could underpin the production for the CSA. I developed promotional materials needed to support the sale of shares, and built a website with the help of my good friend and co-conspirator Seth Seeger. We connected it to PayPal and began taking sign-ups for the inaugural season. I'd envisioned a five-acre mix of 10 grain and bean crops (wheat, oats, corn, barley, rye, spelt, emmer, flax, Tiger Eye, Jacob's Cattle, and Arikara beans) that would provide 25 shares for people in my immediate community. Almost immediately, 50 people signed up, and by the end of the enrollment season we had 90 grain CSA shareholders.

While this was our local response, we were far from alone. As we poured through the web looking for resources and connections to help guide our process, we were stunned by how many others were working on this front. There were burgeoning heritage wheat efforts in France and elsewhere in Europe, as well as in the Pacific Northwest and Alberta, Canada. Vermont, Maine, and New York all supported efforts like ours. There were the Northeast Grain Growers Association, spearheaded by the University of Vermont, and The Bread Lab forming at Washington State University. Even beer was on the line, as malted barley is the primary component, and if folks were going to grow their own bread, you better believe they were going to do the same with their beer. I knew then that this was going to be an incredible adventure.

Heritage Wheat Traditions

Raised Breads

From 1610 to Today

BOILING DOWN THE BAGEL

EASY TO MAKE INCREDIBLE BAGELS AT HOME

The bagel or "Beigel" (meaning ring) originated in the Jewish communities of Poland with records dating back to 1610. The bagel was one of the earliest breads that used the improving quality of the ovens to bake thicker pieces of dough without leaving raw dough in the middle...hence the hole. This was important for two reasons: one, as ovens became more predictable and consistent, it became possible to allow the loaves to "grow taller," allowing a larger quantity of bread in a single bake, which increased efficiency significantly. Also, these little loaves were more transportable and durable than flatbreads, which were more prone to falling apart and going stale; this durability made them a perfect snack or meal on the go, just like we eat them today.

Innumerable different versions of bagels are made around the world, but bagels have been particularly popular in New York and Montreal. New York bagels are chewy and doughy, while Montreal bagels are more crispy and lighter with a larger hole in the middle to maximize 360 degree crispiness. While I personally like them both and welcome bagel style variation I grew up on the chewy, doughy, NY style so this recipe is based on that style.

While boiling is certainly part of many bagel traditions it is also not strictly necessary. When I was doing the research and development for the bagels we produced at Wheatberry we did side-by-side comparisons between the same bagel dough with a steamed versus boiled process and found the difference to be pretty insignificant. A boiled bagel has a slightly sweeter and softer crust due to the honey or malt in the boiling water; the inside or crumb is identical.

Whole Wheat Beigels

The keys to getting this bagel right lies in the stiffness of the dough and the quality of the wheat. This is what lends the chewy, dense crumb of a great morning bagel. The stiffness is also critical if you're going to boil them, because it makes them less fragile and prone to deflating while moving them into the pot.

Ingredients:

1 pound 5 ounces whole wheat flour (or 1lb 6oz sifted)
1/2 teaspoon instant yeast
2 teaspoons salt
2 tablespoons sugar (or 3 tablespoons honey)
15 ounces water at 90 degrees

Directions:

1. Measure out dry ingredients and mix together before adding the water.
2. Warm the water to 90 degrees and mix with the dry.
3. The dough should be a bit stiff and require a little hand kneading to fully incorporate all the flour. It should have a consistency similar to soft clay.
4. Knead for 2-3 minutes in the bowl.
5. Allow to double in size or place in fridge to use the following day.
6. Portion dough into 3 oz squares and then roll into 10 inch strands.
7. After you roll each strand, wrap around your hand with the seam under your palm and roll until even and sealed.
8. If you just want to bake them and skip the boil, top them now. If you are going to boil, top them as they come out of the boil.
9. Place on a baking sheet dusted with flour to proof (rise) until risen 50 percent.
10. Boil in a single layer 1 minute per side and then place on a baking tray with silpat or parchment.
11. Bake for 15-20 minutes at 400 degrees.

SANOK 22/7 1925.
GOTTDANK.

ENGLISH MUFFINS

BUTTER AND JAM, SAUSAGE EGG AND CHEESE, OR EGGS BENEDICT

One of the easiest and most versatile morning breads, English muffins have become a staple in many parts of the world. While they originated in England, it was the Thomas English Muffins, originally known as morning crumpets, that have become the most popular brand and style. That said, if you enjoy English muffins and have never made them at home, you are in for a real treat.

Made with fresh whole ground flour and eaten still warm from the griddle, English muffins are unbeatable satisfying comfort food. Whether you enjoy them simply with butter and jam, sandwiched around sausage, eggs, and cheese, or go the distance and make Eggs Benedict, you will never regret a batch of homemade English muffins. You can keep extras in the freezer for perfect keeping, but good luck getting them in there before they all get eaten. You may want to make a double batch if you want any left over.

Ingredients:

1 pound 5 ounces whole wheat flour (Redeemer or spelt)
1 3/4 teaspoons salt
2 teaspoons instant yeast
1 1/2 tablespoons honey
2 teaspoons white or cider vinegar
2 ounces melted butter or vegetable oil
1 cup water
1 cup milk warmed to 100 degrees

Directions:

1. Mix dry and wet ingredients separately and then combine to form dough.
2. Keep in a warm place (dough should between 76 and 82 degrees).
3. After 30 minutes, fold dough.
4. Allow to double in volume, then scoop with 1/4 cup scoop and round.
5. Rest rounds for 10-15 minutes.
6. Pat or roll rounds into 4-5 inch discs about 1/2 inch thick and place on a baking tray dusted with cornmeal or flour to prevent sticking.
7. After shaping, let muffins rise for another 30 minutes and then griddle both sides on medium heat for about 4 minutes per side. Internal temperature should reach 200 degrees.

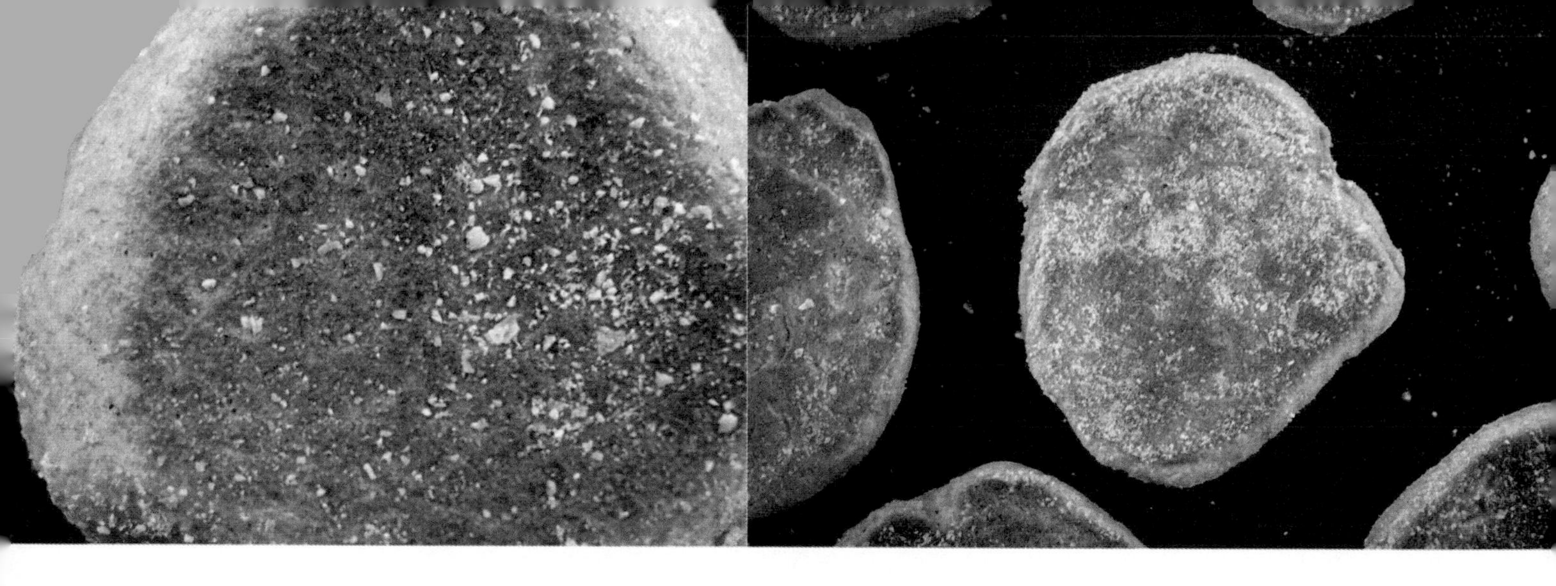

HOLLANDAISE

Hollandaise is quite possibly the most luxurious sauce known to man. Essentially an emulsion of fat and water using the lecithin from eggs as the emulsifying agent, it is a mayonnaise made with butter. It's easy to make but also easy to break, so I have several key tips and tricks to keep your hollandaise smooth and velvety. The easiest way is using the blender method, but a whisk, egg-beater, or handheld immersion blender will get you to the same place. Keep the sauce warm at all times or the butter will congeal, breaking the emulsion. Also be careful not to overheat it, as the eggs could scramble.

Ingredients:

2 whole eggs
1 tablespoon lemon juice or vinegar
1/2 cup unsalted melted butter about 125 degrees
1 teaspoon salt
Hot water as needed

Directions: Blender method

1. Blend the eggs and vinegar on high until doubled in volume. Slowly drizzle in hot butter while blending.
2. Add salt and season with pepper and cayenne to taste and a sprinkle of fresh thyme if you like.
3. Use immediately or put into a preheated thermos to keep for several hours until ready to serve.
5. if it gets too thick, stir in a teaspoon or 2 of water to thin. If it breaks add a little water and re-whip to re-emulsify.

Lotus Leaf Buns

With Red Braised Pork Belly and Black Bean Garlic Sauce

Known as gua bao in its home country, these delectable Chinese steamed buns are often filled with braised pork belly and accoutrements like thinly sliced vegetables, pickled mustard greens, and chopped peanuts.

These soft and springy buns were popularized in America just a few years ago by Asian American restaurants in New York like Momofuko and Bao Haus. Super easy to make and even easier to eat, these can be filled with almost any combo of meat and veggies you can dream up. Paired with hoisin or black bean garlic and chili sauce, you can't go wrong. You can also use the dough to make filled steamed buns. The Yellow Eye beans have a sweet chestnut flavor that makes a great sweet bean filling. Just sweeten the cooked yellow eyes with a little sugar or honey and mash for a sweet filling or use the traditional sweetened red bean paste as is common in China.

I steam these in a bamboo steamer, but any steaming setup will work fine. Put cabbage or spinach leaves under your buns to make cleanup easy and so nothing gets stuck to the bottom of your steamer.

Like any soft buns these use a small amount of fat and sugar (sesame oil and honey in this case) to make the buns soft. The steaming also contributes to the softness of these buns as no crust at all is formed. Fresh out of the steamer, these can't be beat!

Ingredients:

1 pound 6 ounces sifted Redeemer flour

2 teaspoons salt

2 teaspoons instant yeast

1 tablespoon honey

1 tablespoon sesame oil (not roasted) or neutral vegetable oil

2 cups water

Directions:

1. Mix dry ingredients in a mixing bowl.
2. Warm water to 90 degrees and stir in honey and oil.
3. Mix dry and wet ingredients into dough until well combined.
4. Keep in a warm place and allow to double in volume (about an hour).
5. Use a 1/4 cup scoop to portion into rounds.
6. Flatten and roll into an oval 3 inches wide by 6 inches long, brush the inside with oil and fold in half the long way.
7. Place buns into steamer on leaf bed and allow to rise until doubled (30-60 minutes).
8. Steam for ten minutes and then turn off steamer. Allow to cool gently in steamer basket for another 5 minutes before removing.

FRENCH BREAD

THE EXPERIENCE OF TRANSFORMATION

I love the perfect juxtaposition of the ultimately simple yet incredible and nuanced transformation. Ground up grass seeds are taken to one of the greatest culinary heights man has ever reached: French Bread. A crackling, chewy, sweet, and caramelized crust surrounding a moist, irregularly-holed, cool, moist, yielding crumb. Almost any variety of hard wheat will lend its unique characteristic, but this recipe lends itself beautifully to heirlooms such as Red Lammas wheat and Oberkulmer spelt, as well as newer organic varieties such as Redeemer.

Interestingly, you'll note the essential difference between french bread and pita bread is the oven technology. French bread requires an oven that can maintain a relatively even temperature (350-450) for a relatively long time compared to pita. Pitas can be made on a camp fire hearth stone, on a skillet, grill, or even just tossed onto some embers as is still done in some villages today You also can see that the development of ring shaped breads is an intermediate step. As ovens improved like the tandoor oven of India, breads were able to be thicker than pitas, but not in the center, where either a complete hole was made like bagels and sesame rings, or with the center pressed flat and the risen part a circle around the center.

Ingredients:

1lb 5oz Redeemer or Spelt flour

½ teaspoon instant yeast

2 teaspoon fine sea salt

2 cups water at 90 degrees (about 100 in the winter and 65 in the summer)
You may need to adjust the water temperature to correct for very hot conditions in the summer or cold conditions in the winter, but 90 is a good starting place and tends to work for about 8 months of the year.

Directions:

1. Scale and mix your 4 ingredients. The dough mixture should mix together with just a touch of elbow grease, no kneading necessary. The dough should be moist but not wet. It should cling to itself but not stand up tall or tight. Your mixing spoon should cut through the dough without quite picking it up when it is fully mixed. Your dough's temperature should be around 85 degrees.

2. Cover and place in your refrigerator for 6-12 hours. You want it to rise about 50 percent, or from 1 quart of dough to 1.5 quarts. It will work fine if the dough rises as little as 30 percent or as much as 100 percent, but 50 percent is the sweet spot. If your fermentation gets stuck because of poor yeast or cold temperature, you can always add time and warm to move it along. The degree of rise is the most important indicator of dough maturity.

3. Once your primary fermentation is complete, turn your dough out onto a lightly floured work surface. Gently pat out excess gas, allowing some to stay in the dough. Fold and roll the dough into a round or a log, depending on your desired shape; be as creative as you like. Place in your proofing basket.

4. Cover your shaped loaf and return to the fridge for its long, slow final rise. It needs this time to fully develop all its potential character and unlock its optimum keeping and eating quality.

5. 30 minutes prior to baking, preheat your oven to 500 degrees.
Slash and load your fully risen loaf on a sheet pan, in your loaf pan, or onto your baking stone and toss 3 ounces of water onto the bottom of your oven, being careful not to get any on the glass door.

6. Bake for about 40 minutes or until crust is a rich mahogany and the temperature in the center is 200 degrees.

7. Cool for a few seconds and then tear in! The common idea that a loaf can be ruined by cutting in too soon is simply untrue When a loaf comes out of the oven it is fully cooked, or in technical terms the gel has set. The thing to be careful of is wrapping it up while it is cooling, which traps steam being released and makes the crust soggy and encourages mold growth.

Steam Injection

In order for your breads to rise and caramelize(brown) properly you will need to make your oven saturated with steam. The simplest and most effective way to do this is to put 3 ounces of water in a cup. Then you pour the water directly onto your oven floor immediately after loading your breads, followed by quickly closing the oven door. If you do this correctly it will produce so much steam that it will shoot out the cracks and vent holes of your oven. Enough steam will even make your breads shiny! Not enough steam and your breads will look dull and grey and burst out the sides.

At the beginning of the first season, I had arranged to work with White Oak Farm in nearby Belchertown. White Oak Farm had grown grains and beans for many years, mostly as feed for animals. One of the many challenges we faced that first season was finding varieties that would be ideal as human food. While White Oak was a great starting point for this program, it was rife with issues. The owner/operator, was in his seventies and mostly retired. He had an enthusiastic and well meaning understudy, who was alternately devoted to the project and not available or able to complete the critical steps in the process. It was my job to get them seed money and actual seed for the crops, while capturing the action with photography and writing for the website and newsletters. I also had to make sure things were on track for harvest, because I had $30,000 from member shareholders awaiting their grain shares.

We got the fields prepped and crops in the ground, and things were off to a great start. Germination was solid, and we were off. But challenges emerged as the season wore on. Cultivation of the beans was key if we were to harvest the five acres we'd planted. The cultivators needed to be fixed to work the soil. Alas, this didn't happen in time to get the crop properly tilled.

When the beans came ripe, they were too weedy to be harvested by the machine harvester. I began to organize farm shareholders to try to harvest manually. It was a great effort, but a dozen or so people are no match for five acres of beans, and we called it a day after harvesting perhaps a half-acre. We brought in about 300 pounds, when we'd hoped to harvest 3,000 to 5,000 pounds. But all was not lost; The corn was tall, and the wheat, barley, rye, and oats all looked decent. We were not expecting record yields, but the fields had promise. During this time we partnered with NESFI (the host organization for White Oak Farm) and others for a state grant from MDAR to build processing infrastructure for the grains. By the time the crops were ready to come in, we had a refurbished fanning mill to clean and sort the grains. We also had a dehuller to remove the hulls from those grains with hulls, such as spelt, emmer, barley, and oats.

All this grain was to be harvested by an old John Deere 40 combine harvester. The plan was to have it greased and tweaked in time for the harvest. But as the harvest dates neared, the combine was still not up and running. Nearly a week after harvest should have begun, we got the combine out into the fields. It was not too late, but it was too close a call and several crops were lost while other yields were reduced.. While all the efforts made by our first partners were very appreciated, it became clear that this would not be a reliable source of production for the Grain CSA.

Bringing in the crops is just the first half of harvest - grains need to be cleaned immediately before storage. When they come out of the combine, there is a lot of chaff, weed seeds, and other foreign material. You have about 24 hours to get each crop cleaned through the fanning mill and into a storage bin with a large, powerful dryer running; otherwise the crop can literally burst into flames.

With the exception of the beans, we had decent crops that year, but the yields were low. With 90 people signed up, I felt a lot of responsibility to get everyone a great share. A great idea has to have a great product.

Alan Zuchowski, a third generation farmer from Hadley, MA, showed up at the NESFI/MDAR "Grainery" in Belchertown with the Nothstine Dent corn he'd grown and some very high quality Glen bread wheat. He was there to use the new cleaning equipment and had found his market. Alan has been growing for the CSA as our lead farmer ever since. This rounded things out, but didn't account for the beans we needed. I'd been growing beans in the trials and decided I would specialize in growing the beans for the program, since that seemed to be the trickiest crop. We still needed beans for that year's share though, so I began to reach out to farmers in the region to see if anyone was growing any. I found Cayuga Pure Organics out of Cayuga, NY. Not only did they have beans, but they had numerous varieties and other specialty grain crops like emmer and various heirlooms. We had beans, and a great first share.

Along with cooking and baking techniques and recipes that make use of the impressive harvests, this book tells the farmers' stories. It is dedicated to their hard work and commitment, as well as to the willingness of our community to support and embrace this endeavor.

LAZY ACRES FARM - HADLEY, MA

ALAN ZUCHOWSKI

LEAD ORGANIC FARMER FOR THE HERITAGE GRAIN CSA

Crops grown for the CSA: Red Lammas Wheat - Nothstine Dent Corn
Popocorn - Beans - Plymouth Flint Corn

Creating and Maintaining
Sourdough Starter (Levain)

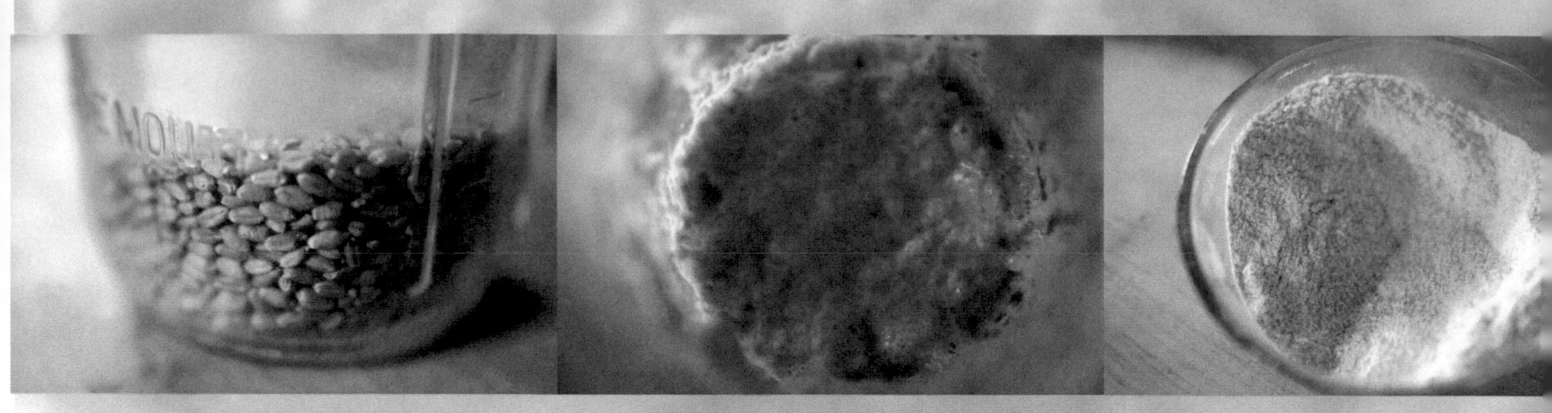

Overview

If you mix flour and water and leave it to sit for several days, it will grow a community of microorganisms and become sour from the lactobacillus present in the air, water, and flour multiplying. If you take a spoonful of the fermented dough and feed it some more water and flour (¼ cup of each), it will ferment again. This is called propagation, but when culturing a starter we usually refer to it as feeding the starter or "levain." It is essential to making sourdough bread; the quality and vitality of your culture is the most important determining factor when making sourdough bread.

Your wild yeast populations need to be very strong and healthy as the lactic acid bacteria won't levain your bread well and you need plenty of active yeasts to create enough gas for your bread to rise sufficiently. A sourdough culture will perform best when it is fed at least once a day, but sometimes cold storage is necessary when you are not baking for more than a few days at a time. It will keep fairly well in the fridge but will need 2-3 days of feeding before it will make high-quality bread again. It's best to keep your starter culture about 68-70 degrees. If it is colder than that the yeast will be very sluggish, and as it gets over 80 degrees it will begin to favor the lactic acid bacteria too much. The warmer it gets, the faster it will multiply (and run out of food).

Getting Started

When starting a sourdough culture (levain) from scratch, it will take about 2 weeks to build up enough healthy yeast, provided it is warm enough and fed daily (except the first 2 days). Once it is active enough (it will be frothing with bubbles and smell like yeast), you can use it every day if you want. Typically, it will get used once or twice a week. In this case ,I recommend feeding it each day for best results. If you are only going to bake with it every other week or once a month, you will want to store it in the fridge and then take it out several days before baking to feed it back to health. 1 teaspoon of active levain can be fed ¼ water and ¼ cup flour each day. A seedling heat mat with a thermostatic probe is a nice way to maintain consistent temperature during the coldest months when you house is likely to be under 65 degrees.

The most important factor in maintaining a healthy levain culture is your ability to determine how "ripe" it is at any given time. Each time you feed the starter culture, it will begin its process of multiplying. When it has consumed most of the available food from a feeding, it will be "ripe" and ready to make bread or be fed again. If you keep feeding your culture at its peak ripeness, it will reward you with a frothing, lively culture that will make very good bread.

So how do you tell when it is at peak ripeness? When you are first building a starter culture, it will be hard to tell since the microbe communities will be small, so be patient at first. As you feed your culture each day, pay close attention to it - smell it, taste it, and notice its appearance. Eventually, you will know from a quick whiff and look. If it is before its peak we call it young, and if it is past its peak we call it old. Anywhere within an hour of peak is desirable. Outside of that range, it will cause your dough fermentation to change considerably and likely lead to less desirable bread.

When you feed your culture, it will look and taste just like water and flour. After a few hours (if your culture is fully active) you will begin to see bubbles forming in the slurry (it's helpful to have a clear container) and after 5-10 hours it will be filled with bubbles. It will smell yeasty with a bit of alcohol and acidity. Somewhere between the 10 and 24 hour marks, the microbes will have consumed most of the available nutrients and will begin to pass its peak ripeness. As this happens, the slurry will begin to break down and separate as large bubbles turn to small ones. The liquid will gradually separate and become increasingly acidic and alcoholic in taste and smell. The more sour your starter becomes, the less suitable for bread making it will be.

It's important to become familiar and comfortable with your levain before making bread with it as it is very discouraging to have a bread failure due to poor starter. If you're not sure if your starter is ready, feed it another day or two. It will be frothing with bubbles when it is ready. Those bubbles are proof of the gas that will generate to raise your bread. If it is not there before you mix your dough, it won't be there in the dough.

All you need is whole wheat flour and water. Yeast are everywhere in our environment and can be gathered from almost any food like grapes or apples, but it is of course present on wheat berries and in wheat flour.

Example feeding schedules:

Starting from scratch

Day 1 - Mix 1/4 cup whole wheat flour and 1/4 cup water (70 degrees).

Day 2 - Nothing.

Day 3 - Take 1 teaspoon from first mix and refeed with 1/4 flour and 1/4 cup water.

Day 4 - Repeat step 3 daily until a frothing yeasty smelling mixture is consistent 12 -24 hours after refeeding.

Once Your culture is looking lively

Once your culture is looking lively It's ready to make sourdough! This will be a 2-3 day process that will only take about 20-25 minutes of work in total. The first day you'll be building your culture so you have enough to levain your bread. Feed it once in the morning and one in the evening. The following morning your starter will will be ready for breadmaking.

If you cold store your culture, make sure to feed it for at least 1 extra day per week it has been in cold storage before using it to make bread.

Example Baker's Math Formulation	Weight	Baker's Math
1. Whole Wheat Flour	595 grams (1lb, 5oz)	100%
2. Water	473 grams (2 cups)	79%
3. Salt	15 grams (1 Teaspoon)	2.5%
4. Yeast	4 grams (1/2 Teaspoon)	0.6%

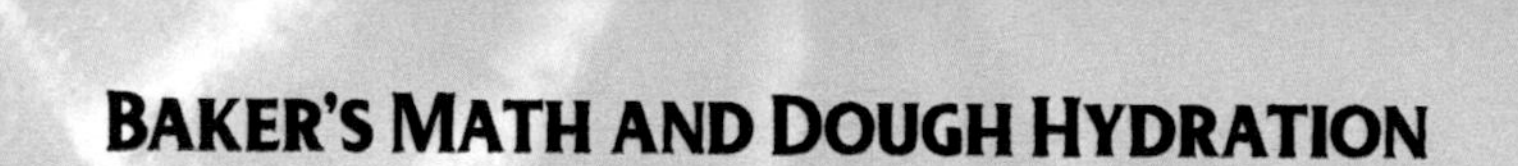

BAKER'S MATH AND DOUGH HYDRATION

Understanding baker's math is a very simple and extremely effective tool for understanding dough hydration (and other aspects of bread formulation). In baker's math, everything is expressed in its relationship to the total amount of flour. The total amount of flour is always equal to 100 percent and everything else is expressed as a percentage in relationship to the flour. So if you have 1000 grams of flour and 700 grams of water (or 7 parts water to 10 parts flour) we would call this 70 percent hydration.

The driest useful dough you can make is around 50% hydration This would be possible to use for pasta, but won't make good bread; its ability to rise would be greatly constricted by excessive elasticity and a lack of extensibility. The driest bread doughs in my repertoire are between 60 and 64 percent hydration and often have a late addition of moisture in the form of added butter, like we see in croissant dough. Most breads will be between 65 percent and 80 percent hydration with enriched doughs generally at the bottom end and lean doughs benefiting from more water. The extra water is important particularly in doughs that have a long fermentation and proofing time since they will slowly dry out during this process.

In the United States, there has been a lot of enthusiasm about using wetter doughs in the past 20 years or so. While these breads do hold up better to long fermentations, they are also significantly stickier and have to be handled with extra skill, care, and lots of dusting flour. They also tend to be weaker structurally, so extra attention is needed to make sure the dough has enough strength to hold on to its rise until it gets all the way to the oven.

SOURDOUGH

PAIN AU LEVAIN - MICHE - RUGBROD - ORINGINAL DELI RYE

OVERVIEW

Before Louis Pasteur discovered yeast with a microscope in 1859, all bread was sourdough. It still took another 100 years for the commercial production of "bread yeast" to begin in earnest. The profound benefits that yeast has had on the quality of our food supply was an ancient phenomenon. Since the benefits of yeast were not understood from a scientific perspective, it was seen as an act of god or magic. That flour and water would turn into rising bread dough or beer without any further effort other than mixing the dough or boiling the soup (wort) was and is an incredible feat.

Blistered, crackling, chewy, bursting crust, dangerously jagged edges (affectionately called ears and grins in french), and a cool, moist crumb with irregular hole structure and a subtle tang. While there are many different styles of sourdough and we'll cover several in this book, I'd like to discuss some of the key features and techniques that lead to varying results.

Sourness/Tang

Sourness is largely determined by the degree of lactobacillus present in the culture. Warmer, longer fermentations generally will lead to more acidity, as these factors favor lactobacilli. It is possible to make sourdough that is puckeringly sour and almost neutral in acidity; it all depends on how you manage your culture. Make it to your liking, but also be aware that moderate acidity will help the bread rise to its fullest possible loft, while both lack of acidity and excess acidity can reduce the breads ability to rise to varying degrees, so it is not just a question of flavor.

Crust Density/Quality

The density or thickness of the crust is impacted by two primary variables: dough leanness and dough density. Breads made without fat and sugar added (lean doughs) are baked at higher temperatures (450 degrees), creating a snappier, chewy crust like we see in French bread and sourdough. Enriched doughs like challah, brioche, and other soft doughs are soft due to the sugar and fat in the dough and are generally baked at about 350 degrees. The density of the dough also has a significant impact on crust quality. For instance, whole wheat bread will be denser than bread made with sifted or white flour and will tend to have a thicker crust due to the longer baking time it will need for the heat to reach the center.

Crust Surface - Smooth vs. Blistered

If you bake your bread within a few hours of shaping the dough, you will have a smooth crust with little to no blistering. However if you cover your shaped dough and place it in the refrigerator for 8-24 hours, it will form many little bubbles on the surface of your dough that will make crunchy little blisters on the surface of your dough. In America blisters are considered very desirable, while in France they are considered a defect. Blistered bread tends to be more tangy due to the longer fermentation which may be behind the preference as the French like their bread less acidic than Americans, generally speaking.

Crumb/Hole Structure

Crumb structure is largely determined by the hydration level of your dough, i.e. the ratio of flour to water. The wetter your dough, the more irregular the size of the holes in your crumb will be. Of course, flour with less bran will still give you more overall loft, but the drier your dough, the more evenly sized the holes will be and vice versa. Ultimately, the profile of your bread will also be affected, as drier doughs make a taller loaf and wetter doughs make a flatter loaf.

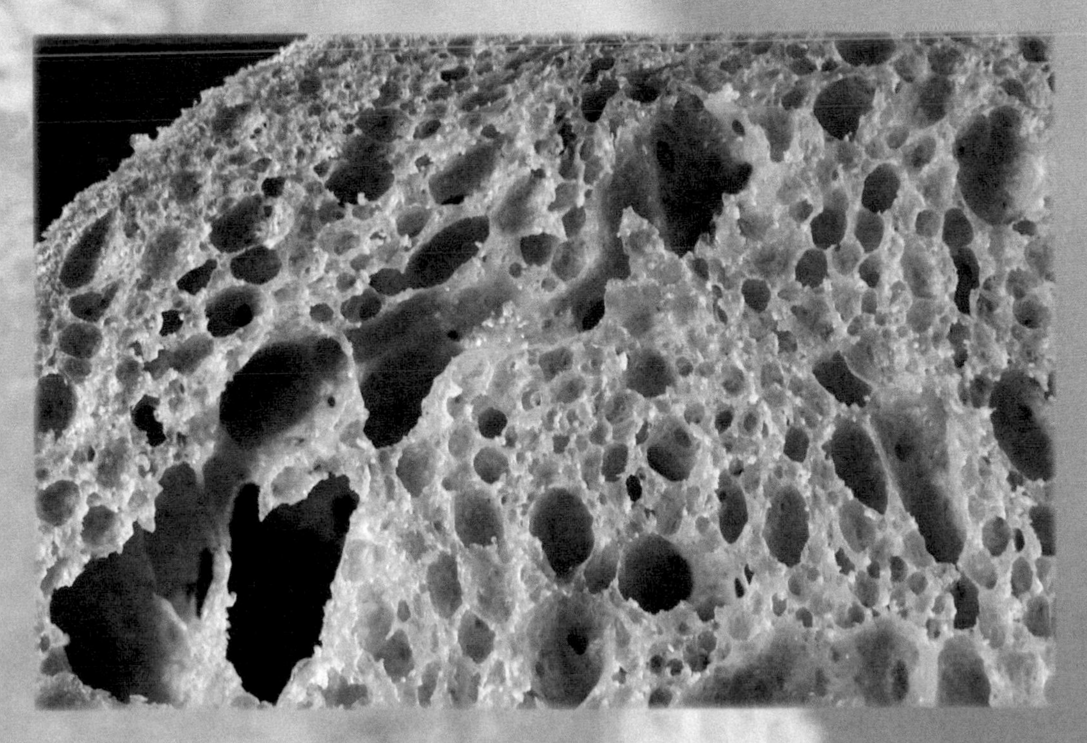

Pain Au Levain

This style of sourdough bread is what opened my eyes to both the aesthetic and transformative sides of bread making. It is simultaneously biology, chemistry, engineering, pleasure, and adventure all at once. That such a seemingly simple ingredient such as wheat flour could grow into a culinary masterpiece enthralled me. Using the wild yeast and lactobacillus culture (called a "starter" or "levain") lends so much depth to the look, flavor, and texture. I'd say pulling a rabbit out of a hat is cute, but transforming a pile of ground up grass seeds into bread is my kind of magic!

When making sourdough, you should have an active and ripe yeast culture that has not over-soured. The more your culture is thriving, the better your bread will be. I can't overstate this! It is important that the temperature of your dough is between 76 and 82 degrees, but you should try for as close to 78 as possible. Depending on the time of year, you will need to adjust your water temperature you mix the dough with, and sometimes the temperature of the space the dough is in too. If your dough is too cool, it will take a very long time to rise and may not rise completely. If your dough is too warm (around 90 degrees), it will rise very fast and could lead to failure from over-rising.

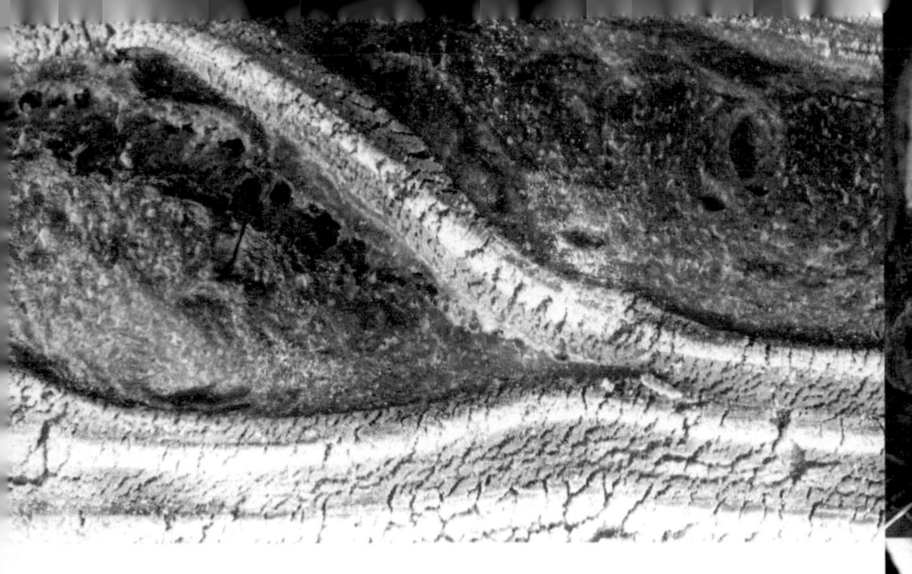

Ingredients:

1lb 7oz Redeemer flour sifted

2 cups water(usually 80-90 degrees spring and fall, 60-70 degrees in the heat of summer, and up to 110 in the cold of winter) you want your dough temperature between 76 and 80 degrees after mixing.

2 teaspoons fine sea salt

1.5 cups whole wheat starter

Directions:

1. Mix your four ingredients together in the container you ferment your dough in. Do not knead your dough -time, folds, and acidity will build all the strength the dough needs. The texture should be neither dry and stiff nor wet and slack but a perfect balance between the two. 67% hydration is the sweet spot (67 parts water to 100 parts flour)

2. Place your dough in a space that is between 76 and 80 degrees. A heat seedling warming mat works well. Alternatively,you can turn your oven on for 2 minutes and then turn it off. Don't let the temperature of your dough drop below 76 degrees or it will likely be compromised

3. Fold your dough after forty minutes.

4. Repeat step two 2-3 times until your dough has risen to 40-60 percent of its original volume. You can use a graduated container to measure the rise. It will go from about 1 quart of dough to 1.5 quarts in size. This is very important.

4. Now that your dough has finished its bulk fermentation, it is ready to shape. The shapes shown here are the (French style boule and Batard risen (proofed) in cane baskets.)

...continued on the next page.

5.The final rise will take about an hour.Alternatively, after 30 minutes you can place the half-proofed loaves into your refrigerator to bake any time in the following 48 hours. Make sure to keep your loaf at about 78 degrees while it is proofing.

6. Preheat your oven for 30 minutes to 450 degrees. Bake until the temperature in the center of the loaf is 200 degrees. After loading the bread, pour about 2-3 ounces of water right onto the bottom of your oven and close the door immediately. This will produce the steam essential for your bread to rise and caramelize during the bake properly.

7. If the top isn't browning as fast as the bottom, move the loaf higher in the oven. If the loaf is browning too quickly on the bottom, add another sheet pan under it.urn as needed for even browning.

8. Cool on a wire rack for several hours and slice for eating as fast as possible. Bread is best still hot from the oven...don't listen to the bread curers unless you're packaging in plastic. If you want to put your bread in a sealed bag or container, wait 24 hours to do so to allow excess moisture to dissipate that would spoil your loaf in a sealed environment. If you want your bread to last a week, put it in the fridge after 2-3 days.

2-3 hours on a wire rack
then to paper bag for 24 hours
then to plastic bag or bread bin for 36 hours
and then to fridge for 5 days
or slice and freeze anytime and keep for several months.

It is hard to wait for a starter to get fully ripe and active before use, since it can take up to a couple of weeks. This photo is of a loaf I made from my starter at about ten days in, and while it was bubbling it clearly wasn't completely at its fullest potential. I made bread anyway and while the bread isn't as well risen or aesthetically pleasing it was perfectly tasty. Compare with the pictures of the same loaf made with starter that was fully active at about 14 days(previous page). Remember this only applies to a new starter culture. If you have an active culture already you can build your starter one day and bake with it the next. If you have an active culture that has been in the refrigerator, make sure to feed it for 2-3 days until is is clearly bubbling away at a good pace.

MICHE

Whole Wheat Sourdough

These enormous dark and crusty loaves can be made any time you like. They don't have to be big, but they are at their best when they are a larger loaf. The balance of flavors and textures, the tangy, cool, and moist crumb, and the chewy, dark molasses crust make for a delicious bread.

Each miche is unique in the type and character of the wheat used in it, as well as the type and character of the starter culture It is a standard by which wheat can be judged for its bread baking suitability if you are experienced enough to judge this. The Redeemer wheat makes an unbearably delicious example of this bread style.

Ingredients:

3 cups starter

2 pounds 12 ounces whole fresh wheat flour("Redeemer" is my favorite)

4 cups warm water

4 teaspoons fine sea salt

Directions:

1. Prepare 3 cups of starter (levain) over two feedings the day before (see p. xx).
2. When the levain is at peak ripeness, add 2 pounds and 12 ounces of whole meal flour (ideally fresh ground), 4 teaspoons fine sea salt and 4 cups warm water (80-90 degrees in the spring and fall, 100-110 in the winter, and 70 in the heat of summer). You want your dough above 76 and below 85 degrees, aiming for 78 degrees.
3. Ferment for 30 minutes and then fold.
4. Repeat step 3.
5. Flour the top of the dough and turn out onto a floured work surface. Gently fold and round and place on a baking tray to proof for 30-40 minutes.

6. Preheat your oven to 450 while the loaf is proofing and get 3 ounces of water ready to place into the bottom of the oven when you load the loaf.
7. When the loaf has risen by about 30 percent, which should take about 30-40 minutes, slash the loaf and load the oven with water for steam. Bake for 20 minutes and then turn. Check for evenness of bake and move loaf accordingly for even baking throughout.
8. Once an internal temperature of 200 degrees is reached and the loaf is browned as desired, place on a cooling

RUGBROD

DANISH WHOLE RYE WITH FLAX AND SUNFLOWER SEEDS

This type of rye bread is common across much of eastern Europe, as rye is better suited to those climates than wheat. Dense, dark, and tangy with complex earthy flavors, whole rye breads are quite different than wheat breads, both in the making and the final result. Rye is very high in Amylase enzymes, which causes it to ferment much faster, reducing bulk or primary fermentations by 75 percent compared to its wheat counterparts. Because the balance of gluten proteins is different than wheat, it has a significantly less structure to trap gas and therefore rises less. Rye dough is actually more like a very thick pancake batter. The rye chops are mixed with water, some of the flour, and the starter 24 hours before mixing the dough. Once the dough is mixed, it bulk ferments for 30-45 minutes and then goes into the pan for its final rise, another 30-45 minutes. The bake starts hot but then goes low to let the heat penetrate to its center without over-baking the outside. It is meant to be sliced thin and eaten with all manner of cheeses, spreads, or smoked meats, to name a few. It density allows it to keep much longer than wheat breads without going stale.

Ingredients:

1 cup cracked wheat
1 cup cracked rye
1/2 cup flaxe seeds
1/2 cup sunflower seeds
1 tablespoon molasses
1.5 cups sourdough starter
3.5 cups water
1.5 cups wheat flour
1.5 cups rye flour
1 tablespoon salt

Directions:

1. Put the first 7 ingredients in a large mixing bowl and allow to soak and ferment for 12 to 24 hours
2. Add the remaining ingredients and ferment in a warm place for 1.5 hours
3. Divide the dough into two bread pans and let rise for 1-2 hours until it has risen 30-50% in volume
4. Bake the breads for about 1 hour at 360 degrees until the temperature in the center reaches 200 degrees
5. When finished baking remove the breads from the pan and allow to fully cool. Store in airtight container in your fridge for up to 2 weeks or indefinitely in your freezer.

SHCHI

Ingredients:

1 green cabbage
1 jar of sauerkraut
2, 16 ounce jars of tomatoes
2 medium onions(red is nice for the color it adds)
2 pounds of chuck stew beef
1 cup cider vinegar
Salt and pepper to taste

Directions:

Add all the ingredients to a large pot and simmer gently until the beef is tender.Serev immedientely or Put in your refrigerator for up to one week. As with most stews and soups the flavors improve and develop over time.

ORIGINAL DELI RYE
WITH CARAWAY SEEDS AND PASTRAMI

Created and made famous by the Jewish delicatessens of New York City, this bread typically contains only 20-30 percent rye flour; the remaining is wheat flour. It gets its most distinctive characteristic from the caraway seeds. The rye flour is fermented with sourdough starter, which lends a bit of the more traditional rye flavor, similar to a rugbrod or other whole rye sourdoughs. A soft crust and a tender, even crumb combined with the more assertive flavors of caraway and sourdough rye makes this bread the perfect accompaniment to smoked and cured meats like pastrami or smoked whitefish.

Ingredients:

14 ounces Sifted Redeemer Flour
8 ounces whole rye flour
1/2 cup starter
1 tablespoons sugar
2 teaspoons caraway seeds
2 teaspoons salt
1 teaspoon instant yeast
12 ounces water

Directions:

1. In a large mixing bowl mix together all the dry ingredients
2. Warm the water to 100 degrees (unless it is summer use 70-80)
3. Mix the dry and wet together and knead into a soft but not wet dough. ideal dough temperature is about 80 degrees.
4. Keep in a warm place and ferment for 30-60 minutes until it has increased in volume about 50%
5. Fold dough to degass and strengthen it's structure
6. Ferment for another 30-60 minutes for another 50% size increase
7. When risen turn dough out onto a flour dusted work surface and pat into a round
8. Fold and round dough into ball shape and place in a banneton or towel lined bowl
9. Allow to rise 50-75% involume(45-90 minutes) and then turn out onto a baking sheet with a silicone mat or a dusting of flour.
10. preheat your oven to 400 degrees for 25 minutes and bake loaf until internal temperature reads 200. About 45 minutes
11. When loading the loaf make sure to toss 3-4 ounces of water in the bottom of your oven to steam the loaf ensuring a proper rise and caramelization of the crust.

Note: this loaf can also be shapoed into a log and proofed and baked in a loaf pan for a rectangular shape.

Season 2 was an exciting year. With such a substantial membership and interest in the first shares, I was pumped for a second season. While I had made some great new connections with farmers who could help supply the grain share, I decided to hone in on bean production myself as this seemed the most challenging aspect of the project.. Our beans had failed the first year, but I was determined to get a bean crop all the way to distribution on this second go around.

My property in Shutesbury had about a half of an acre cutivatable, so I decided to rent a field around the corner from my house from a neighbor. I enlisted the help of my good friend Seth Seeger as my partner in farming, as well as the power and drive of a new friend Cole. A 1,600 pound draft horse. If you'd like to see a 10-second clip of our cultivations with cole you can watch it at www.localgrain.org/cole-video

I could pull on my crew from the Bakery and folks from the membership for peak moments, but generally Seth, Cole, and I were on the job. We worked hard to get the field prepped in time for an early June planting. Without a proper corn planter, we used a group of five to seed the crop with small push seeders. The first two cultivations we did with Cole and a walk behind and ride behind cultivator. The third pass was with a small crew to rogue the field by hand one last time and get things ready for a smooth harvest. The final harvest would be with a crew of about eight to pull the beans and load them into a huge cart we had built, attached to the back of a tractor. Then we brought them to my place where we erected a hoop house in the face of a massive rainstorm that threatened our crop. We strapped the plastic sheet to the top of the hoop house literally minutes before the rain came down in a deluge.

This is the inevitable drama of farming, and it doesn't always have a happy ending like this one. It is fraught with hard work and investments that don't pay off. While we did get a gorgeous crop of heirloom beans in (Arikara, Tiger Eye, and Jacob's Cattle), it was not terribly cost effective. We had about 500lbs and it cost us around $3,000-4,000 to produce. In hindsight this wasn't too bad for a first/second attempt but it was a lot to take on at the time; I was still running the bakery with a staff of 12 and many constant demands.

Alan continued to grow the Glen Wheat while taking over the corn production for the share, his specialty. He grew Mandan Bride, Nothstine Dent, popcorn, and Blue Hopi. He also began expanding the seed supply for the Red Lammas wheat he would eventually grow to a commercial scale. He also grew spelt and tried flax as well.

This was also the time that Stan and Abbie White and their two sons came into the picture. They had started out attempting to grow barley for beer production, but discovered that wheat was much better suited to their farm. They were growing the Redeemer wheat and it was a real winner as far as flavor, yield, and quality for making all manner of bread. This was the beginning of a long and fruitful partnership for the share. The White Family would eventually build a mill house that would provide us with local flours from local grains.

The second year we also connected with two other new and future partners. The first was Sara and Matt Williamson of Aurora Farm and Mill in Maine. They specialize in oats and have become our farm for whole oat groats, steel cut, and rolled raw oats. They are a pleasure to work with and grow the finest oats I have ever had the good fortune to enjoy.

The other connection was a chance meeting with Erik Andrus of Boundbrook Farm. I was attending an heirloom wheat growing seminar where Erik and I connected as fellow bakery owners involved in growing wheat for our bakeries. He explained that he was experimenting with rice because his farm seemed too wet for consistent, high-quality wheat crops. At the time a good number of folks were experimenting with rice production, but Erik struck me as the most likely to pull it off.

JOHN DEERE
720

Around this time, we had successfully applied for a SARE grant of our own to help document and share the work we were doing. When we applied, the grant was for $25,000 but after we were awarded the grant the budget was cut to $15,000 as a result of the Great Recession. It finally hit our bakery business that winter and cut our sales back a whopping 30 percent. This was just after the cost of grains had risen by threefold the spring before. This is not an easy way to start a business.

CHALLAH

WHOLE WHEAT POPPY AND SIFTED SESAME

Challah is a very special and ancient bread. Originating in Jewish culture, it is still very important in modern Sabbath traditions as well as the major Jewish holidays today. Enriched with eggs and honey or sugar and often topped with sesame or poppy seeds, this style of bread has become popular all around the world, both within and outside the Jewish community. Eggs have a unique effect on bread dough, as the yolk and the white each contribute special characteristics to the dough. Eggs are high in lecithin, which improves dough texture and helps prevent the bread from going stale. This soft and rich bread works well in many different scenarios.

Whether you're serving challah as part of the Sabbath with a sprinkling of salt or whipping up some challah french toast over the weekend, there are endless ways to prepare it. It makes both fantastic sandwiches or as little toast points with fancy toppings for a brunch - it is a great bread to experiment with. You can also add raisins to the dough and it can even be used to make excellent babka by adding chocolate and spices to the mix.

I also like to make a brioche/challah hybrid which makes an incredible version, albeit not a traditional or kosher loaf. To do this, just replace the oil with butter. I hope this doesn't offend any staunch traditionalists, but as much as I love and honor tradition I never stop experimenting with anything that might taste incredible.

Ingredients:

1 pound 5 ounces sifted or whole wheat flour
1 tablespoon instant yeast
2 teaspoons fine sea salt
8 ounces water(9 for whole wheat)
2 whole eggs and 2 yolks
1/3 cup honey
4 tablespoons vegetable oil

Directions:

1. Mix together the dry ingredients in a mixing bowl
2. Warm water to 110 degrees, and then stir in the honey and oil, then the eggs and yolks
3. Add wet ingredients to the mixing bowl and combine thoroughly with the dry mix
The dough should be about 80 degrees after mixing. Anything under 76 degrees will really slow down the rise
5. Keep in a warm place and allow to fully double in volume (45-90 minutes)
6. Once doubled, deflate and portion into balls with 1/4 cup scoop and round
7. Cover rounded dough balls and allow to rest for 20-25 minutes
8. Roll the dough balls into 12-inch tapered logs and braid
Note: There are too many ways to braid dough too cover in this, but a quick Google search will get you the braiding patterns for a variety of styles, such as 3, 4 ,5, 6 and even 12-strand braids
You can even learn to braid multiple loaves together for some incredible presentations
11. Once your loaf (or loaves) are braided, cover and allow to double in volume before baking
12. Preheat your oven to 350 degrees 20 minutes before baking
13. Once your loaves are risen, brush with egg wash,top with your favorite seeds, and bake to an internal temperature of 200 degrees
15. Cool on a wire rack and enjoy...challah is best still steaming from the bake!

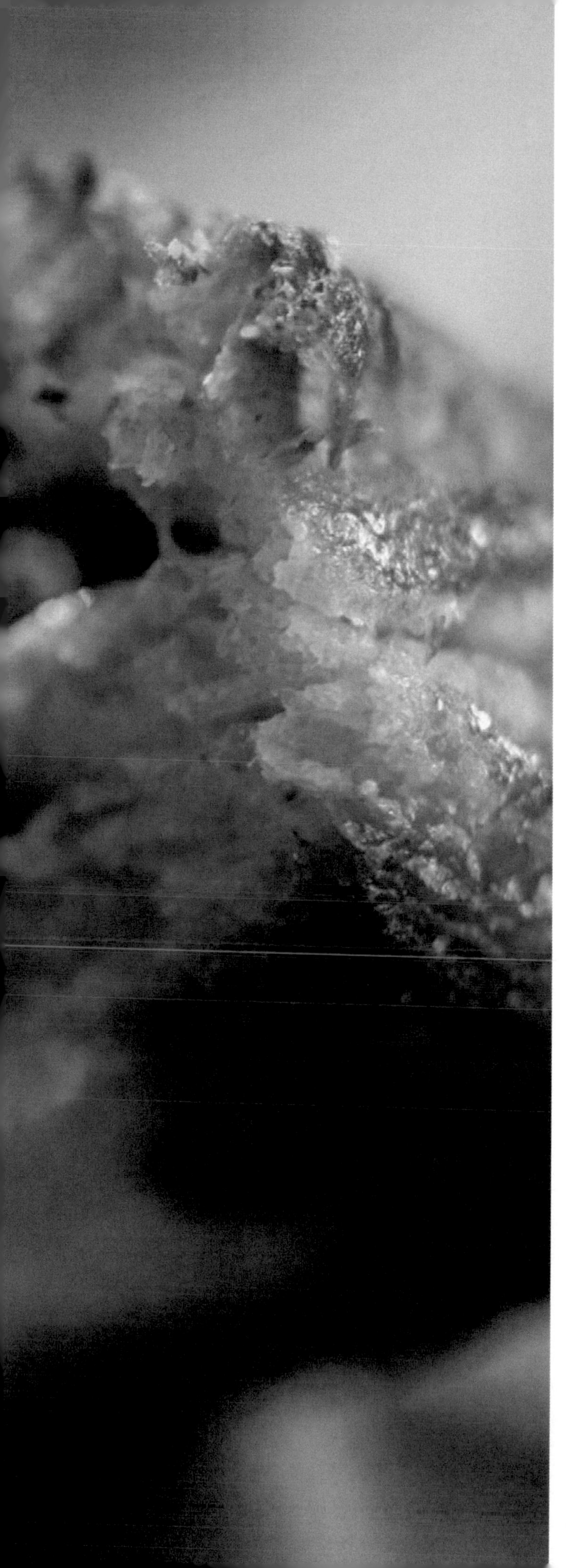

HERITAGE WHEAT TRADITIONS

PASTRY

SWEET ENRICHED TREATS TO DIE FOR

The Whole Wheat Cherry Scone

My spin on the humble scone
and
the surprising result

Croissants

Lamanation
Chocolatine
and Variations

Cookies

Classic Chocolate Chip

Triple Chocolate

Cakes and tarts

Boston Cream Pie

Apple Tart

Chocolate Cake with
Peanut Butter Frosting

Raspberry Galette

Whole Wheat Cherry Scones

These crispy, crumbly, buttery scones have a surprising allure that few breads can match. In all honesty, I am not a huge scone fan personally, but I developed this recipe early on in the development of Wheatberry and they really struck a chord with a lot of people. We made 40 quarts of scone dough 3-6 times a week for almost 10 years; that was only limited because we decided to stop wholesaling our goodies in 2008 so we could focus on the in-house production and make the space to create the grain CSA.

The technique to make this scone is a bit different than most, as you cut the butter similar to how you would for a shortbread or pie dough. That is a big part of what makes these so special, yielding a perfect texture. The dried sweetened cherries come from Michigan and also add a very special sweet and sour chew that caramelizes a bit on the edges.

You can do the mixing in a large mixing bowl, a food processor, or a stand mixer. This recipe will make one large disc that can be sliced into 6 large scones. Alternatively, each large scone can be cut into three triangles for 18 mini scones. These are not low calorie, so think of a large scone as a meal and a mini scone as a little treat. You can shape them any way you like, but this recipe details how we made them at our bakery. The dough also keeps very well in the freezer, so don't hesitate to make extra to have on hand for a quick treat or breakfast!

Ingredients:

8 ounces whole wheat flour

3 ounces cane sugar(I like to use turbuinado for a touch of extra flavor)

1/2 teaspoon baking powder

2 teaspoons Baking soda

3/4 teaspoon salt

4 ounces butter

4.5 ounces oats

4 ounces dried sweetened cherries

4.25 ounces buttermilk(or 3 ounces yogurt and 1.25 ounce water)

Directions:

1. Measure out all ingredients first

2.Mix the first 5 ingredients together. Make sure the baking powder and baking soda are fresh and not clumpy; sift as needed.

2. Place your cold butter on a work surface and pound flat with a rolling pin. Chop into small pieces (dust with a little flour from the dry mix to keep pieces separate.)

3. Add the dry mix and butter to your machine or mixing bowl. If using a machine, mix the butter and flour together until butter clumps are gone and it resembles sand. Do not mix it long enough to form a dough.

If you are mixing in a bowl, the easiest way to incorporate the butter and rye mix is to use your hands and squish the two together. Mix until there are no more butter clumps and it resembles sand, do not form a dough.

5. Add the cherries and oats and stir to combine evenly

6. Add the buttermilk. If using a machine, run it just until a dough forms and then stop If mixing in a bowl, use your hands to compress the dough together.

8. Form into your preferred shape and bake at 350 until just set, about 20-25 minutes

REAL
BUTTER
MILK
CULTURED
GRADE A • PASTEURIZED
From Fresh Cream
Churned into Butter
Farm Made in Maine
Less Than 1% Milk Fat
NOT made from skim milk
Contains active yogurt cultures
16 FL. OZ. (473ml)

CROISSANTS
PAIN AU CHOCOLATE AND VARIATIONS

Layers upon layers of buttery, soft dough sheets, surrounded by crispy outer layers of the same...what's not to love? I suppose the downside is that it takes about 3 days to make from start to finish, and requires some level of skill in handling the dough. When I started Wheatberry Bakery, sourdough was the core bread and croissants were the core pastry. For many years I worked hard at creating the perfect croissant. The outer layers are explosively crispy while the inner layers are soft and stretchy with a subtle yeasty tang to balance the richness of the butter. While the very first batch I made was delicious, it took about 3 years of commercial production to perfect and stabilize the process so I could show others how to make them.

Ingredients:

1 pound 5 ounces Redeemer flour
2 ounces sugar
2 teaspoons instant yeast
2 teaspoons fine sea salt
3-8 ounces of scrap dough trimmings from the previous batch(optional)
8 ounces water
8 ounces milk

***You will also need 12 ounces of butter for the lamination**

100% WHOLE WHEAT PAIN AU CHOCOLATE

Directions:

1. Mix dry ingredients in a large mixing bowl
2. Combine the water and milk and warm to 100 degrees
3. Mix the wet and dry ingredients together thoroughly to make the base dough
4. For the primary fermentation, when using sifted flour the dough should nearly triple in size twice. So if you have 1.2 quarts of dough it should rise to 3 quarts.hen de-gass and repeat. If you are using whole wheat flour, it should also rise twice but only double in volume
6. Once the primary fermentation is complete, the dough should be rolled out into a rectangle on a sheet pan about 1.5-2 inches thick.
7. Refrigerate for 30-45 minutes
8. Roll out one more time just to remove any gas (do not fold it at this point)
9. Place your dough into the freezer
10. At this point the dough will be ready to laminate with the butter the next day once the dough has had a chance to rest. It will also keep in the freezer up to 2 weeks
11. When you are ready to laminate the dough, take it out of the freezer to defrost.You will want to laminate while the dough is still very cold but just above freezing
13. While the dough is defrosting, get your butter out and pound with a rolling pin to make it pliable. Shape the butter into a rectangle half the size of your dough rectangle
14. If your dough is still defrosting when you finish preparing the butter, put your butter in the fridge to stay cool while you wait for the dough, and vice versa - if your dough is getting too soft while you prepare the butter, put it back in the freezer to hold its chill.

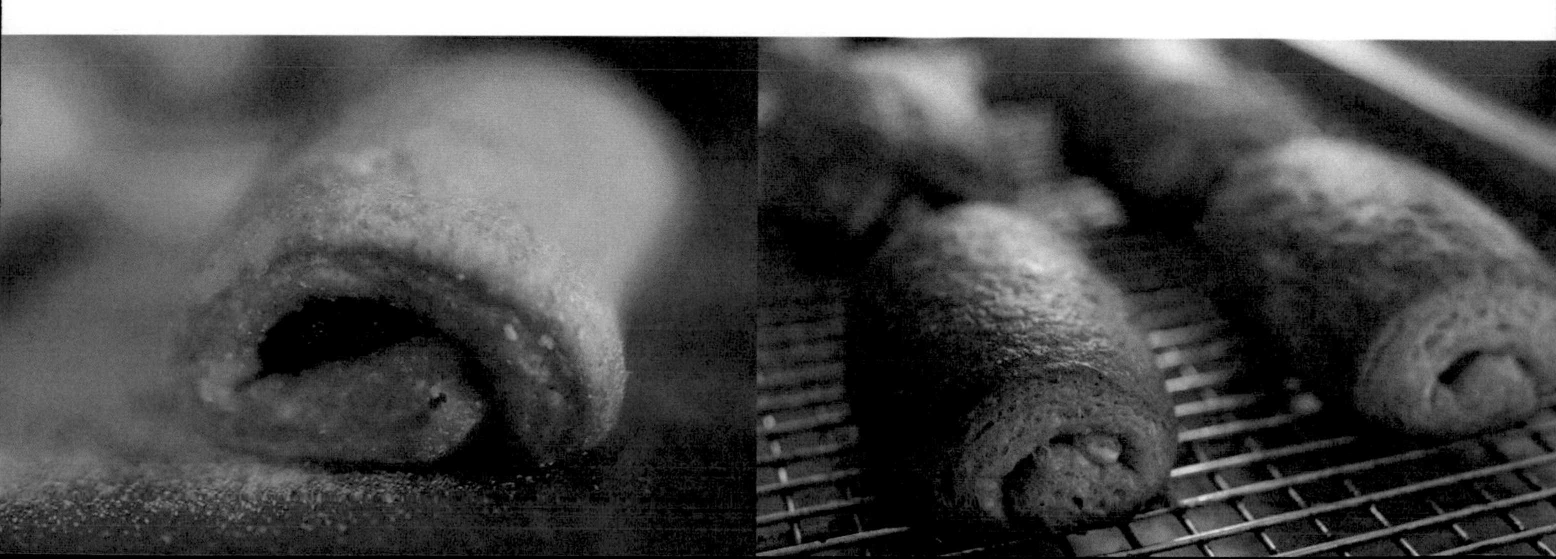

ORGANIC SWEET CREAM
UNSALTED BUTTER
NET WT 4OZ (113g)

15. For the lamination, you want the butter and dough to be cold and stiff, and as close to the same stiffness as possible while still malleable.
16. Once your dough and butter are both ready, place the butter rectangle on top of the dough rectangle and fold the dough over the butter as if closing it in a book.
17. Pinch the sides closed so the butter doesn't leak out during the lamination
18. Once the butter is sealed in the dough you can use a large rolling pin to press the layers together and get the dough and butter moving together. If one is too much softer than the other they won't roll together, so consistency is key.
19. Roll the dough in the long direction until it is 3 times as long as it is wide,
then fold the dough in a letter fold
21. Place back in the fridge for 30-60 minutes
22. After the dough has rested in the refrigerator, roll again, shifting the process 90 degrees (If you continue rolling the dough in the same direction, it won't work.) Roll it 3 times as long as it is wide and do a letter fold.
23. Once the lamination is complete,rest the dough in the refrigerator for 1-3 hours
24. After this final rest, the dough can be rolled out one more time until it is 1/4 inch thick evenly across the sheet. Rest the dough in the fridge one more time for 15-30 minutes and then bring out to fine tune the sheet and cut your shapes to make the croissants.

COOKIES

Based on historical texts, cookies seem to have originated in the 7th century AD in Persia, where the use of sugar had become common. By the 14th century, cookies were commonplace throughout Europe. These calorie-dense cookies were made on the hard side so they could travel well. Cookies made their way to the United States by the 1700s by way of the Dutch, anglicizing their word "koekje" into cookie.

Variations on the cookie are quite literally endless. I try to cover some of my favorites and a few different variations, but the recipes in this book are just the tip of the iceberg. The dough for these recipes keep very well in the freezer and can be baked as needed. Dough can be stored in a freezer bag either in a log or a flat rectangle, depending on your desired shape. They can also be portioned individually using a portion scoop and then frozen.

Easy to make and whipped up in a matter of minutes, you can't argue with a cookie. As long as your leavener is fresh and sifted and you mix your dry ingredients before combining with the wet, you have great results time after time. You can also play around with recipe proportions and see what new cookie creations you can add to the matrix.

Classic Chocolate Chip

Ingredients:

1.5 cups whole wheat flour
1/2 teaspoon baking soda
1/4 teaspoon salt
4 ounces softened butter
1/2 white sugar
1/2 cup brown sugar
1 large egg
1 teaspoon vanilla extract
1.5 cups semi sweet chocolate chunks or chips

Directions:

1. Mix flour, salt and baking soda(sift soda) in a large mixing bowl
2. Cream butter and sugar together
3. Add the egg and vanilla extract to creamed mixture and combine
4. Fold the two mixtures to combine
5. When the cookie batter is almost mixed stir in the chocolate chips
6. Bake at 350 for 10-15 minutes or freeze in a log or prescooped indefintely

Triple Chocolate

Ingredients:

7 ounces whole wheat flour
1/3 cup cocoa powder
1/4 teaspoon baking powder
1/4 teapooon baking soda
1/4 teaspoon salt
1 cup sugar
5 ounces butter
1 teaspoon vanilla extract
1 large egg
1 cup semi sweet chocolate chips
1 cup white chocoalte chips or chunks

Directions:

1. Mix the first 5 ingredients passing the leveners through a sieve
2. Melt the butter and stir in the sugar
3. Add the vanilla extract and the egg(make sure the butter is not too hot or it will scrable your egg)
4. Combine your wet and dry mixes and stir to combine adding the chips when 2/3 the way mixed.
5. Once the flour streaks are just gone your cookie dough is ready. Bake for ten to 15 minutes at 350

CHOCOLATE CAKE
WITH PEANUT BUTTER FROSTING

I have come to believe that most shortbread, cakes, cookies, etc. are best made with whole wheat flour. There are several reasons for this. Most importantly, whole wheat flour is less likely to become doughy due to the extra bran and germ. This makes for a "shorter" bread with better texture. Also, while whole wheat pastries rise perfectly well, they are slightly denser than those made with sifted or white flour. This keeps them more moist when they come out of the oven and as they sit. Less air on the inside means slower oxidation and will keep for longer. The extra flavor from the bran and germ also tends to balance well with the sweetness of pastry. Lst but not least, keeping the bran and germ makes sweet things healthier so you can feel less guilty, eat more, and have better digestion.

Ingredients:

3 cups whole wheat flour
1/2 cup cocoa powder
1 tsp. baking soda
1/2 tsp Baking Powder
1 tsp. salt
2 cups sugar
2/3 c. butter(melted) or vegetable oil
2/3rd cup yogurt
2 tsp. vanilla(optional)
1 cup milk or water

Directions:

1. Mix together the first 6 ingredients in a large mixing bowl
2. Add wet ingredients and stir until just combined
3. Pour batter into a well greased and floured pan. A 9-inch springform works perfect or 9x13 square will work as well - just add parchment paper to the bottom to aid removal
4. Bake at 350 for 30-35 minutes
5. The most important thing with a cake like this is to bake it just until it reaches an internal temperature of 200 degrees. Baking it any hotter than that will dry it out.

PEANUT BUTTER FROSTING

Ingredients:

Beat together:
¼ lb. butter
1 ½ cups of peanut butter
1 tsp. vanilla
Add and mix on a slow speed of electric mixer or food processor:
1 lb. Confectioners sugar
Gradually add:
At least 1/3 cup to ½ cup milk – sometimes takes more – you want a light fluffy frosting that will spread easily. When chilling, both the butter and the peanut butter will harden and stiffen the frosting. This will make enough for a 9x13 cake. Cut the recipe in half for an 8 inch cake.

BOSTON CREAM PIE

WITH MAPLE CUSTARD AND SEASONAL FRUIT

The original Boston Cream Pie (actually a cake) was developed by a French chef at the Parker House Hotel in Boston in the late 1800s and was originally originally named chocolate cream pie. Growing up, my first introduction to Boston Cream Pie was via the still popular Boston Cream Pie doughnut. Since that is a very impractical thing to make at home, mostly due to the combination of deep frying and then filling, the original version is fairly simple and just as delicious...maybe better!

The original cake used was a sponge cake, but as sponge cakes tend to be dry out, I prefer a simple butter cake, which are much faster and simpler to make. The original chocolate on top was fondant, but here we will use a ganache for improved flavor and texture.

Here I am adding seasonal fruit to add another layer, but this is completely optional. The custard is simple vanilla, but you can always get creative with how the custard is flavored, too.

Ingredients: The Butter Cake

Dry

1.5 cups flour

1 cups sugar

½ tsp baking soda

1/4 teaspoon baking powder

1/4 tsp salt

Wet

2 eggs

1 tsp vanilla extract

½ cup butter

3/4 cup milk or water

Directions:

1. Mix the dry ingredients thoroughly in a large mixing bowl, sifting the leaveners
2. Melt the butter and whisk together with the other wet ingredients (making sure not to scramble the eggs)
3. Preheat oven to 350 degrees
4. Butter and flour a 9 inch springform pan or similar.
5. Add the wet mix to the dry and fold together with a spatula until just combined
6. Pour batter into your prepped pan and bake until set and the cake's temperature reaches 200 degrees.

CHOCOLATE GANASH

1/4 cup heavy cream

1 cup semi sweet chocolate

1 tsp vanilla(optional)

Heat in a small sauce pan until just melted through. Allow to cool for about one hour before frosting cake as it will be too liquid when very hot.

VANILLA/MAPLE CUSTARD

Ingredients:

2 cups water(or milk)

1/2 cup maple syrup

¼ cup sugar

¼ tsp salt

1/4 cup cornstarch

¼ cup tapioca starch

3 eggs

Directions:

1. Put the cornstarch in the bottom of a medium-sized saucepan and add just enough water to hydrate (¼ cup). Add the rest of the ingredients all at once and begin to whisk hard, adding just enough water to make a thick paste.
2. Gradually add more water until the mixture starts to loosen,then add the rest, whisking well to combine. Turn heat to high and constantly whisk as the mixture heats. It will begin to steam around 140 degrees and then start to thicken and gelatinize around 170-80 degrees.
3. Whisk hard as the mass becomes thick and difficult to stir. Continue to stir hard for 1 minute while the starches fully gelatinize.
4. Remove from heat and put one teaspoon of custard on a plate and into the fridge to chill. Once cooled, you can check what the room temperature viscosity will be.
5. If it is not thick enough, mix 2 tablespoons cornstarch and 2 tablespoons water into a slurry and pour into the custard while whisking. Simmer for another minute,remove from heat, and repeat fridge test.
6. Allow custard to cool and use when room temperature or cooler.

Apple Tart

Shortcrust doughs became common in medieval Europe during the mid 1500s, 200 years after the pie became common. A basic pie or tart dough is an awesome thing to have on hand. It is useful both for sweet and savory applications as well as closed or open pies and tarts. This apple tart I learned in an early restaurant position I held where the French chef taught me how to make this. It is simply made by turning some apples into applesauce, rolling out and blind baking a tart shell, filling the tart shell with the apple sauce, and topping with sliced apples for the bake.

While it is most common to use white flour to make this type of shortcrust, I prefer whole wheat, which makes a more tender crust and adds more depth of flavor to any pie or tart. It requires a slightly different approach. With a white flour crust, it is really important not to overwork it or it will make a tough crust. With whole wheat, it is the opposite - if you don't work the dough enough, it will be too delicate to roll out and shape into your baking mold. If you go to roll it out and it falls apart, just ball it up and start again until it is manageable. It may need 5 minutes to rest after being balled up.

Ingredients:

For the tart shell -

2.5 cups whole wheat flour
1/2 teaspoon salt
8 ounces butter
1-2 tablespoons water
For the filling -
6 medium sized apples
Sugar, honey or maple syrup
Cinnamon
Vanilla extract

Directions:

1. The simplest way to make this dough is to put all the ingredients in a food processor and blitz it up for 30-60 seconds.
2. As described in the scone recipe, you can also cut the butter in by hand or in a stand mixer.
3. Once mixed, dust generously with flour and shape the dough into 44-oz discs about 5-6 inches wide and 1/2 inch thick. This makes them easy to roll out.
4. Place in the fridge to chill and relax for at least one hour or overnight. They can be kept frozen and ready for use indefinitely.
5. After the dough has chilled, roll out into a 12 -inch circle and line a 9-inch fluted tart pan.
6. Prick the bottom of the crust all over with a fork to minimize bubbles
7. Bake for 20-25 minutes or until golden brown at 350 degrees
8. Make apple sauce. Chop apples into a sauce pan and add sugar and spices. Depending on how sweet or tart your apples are, use more or less sugar and add lemon juice for extra zing.
9. When your tart is baked and your apple sauce is cooked, slice your apples to go on top. Using a mandoline for this will get you thinner, more even slices that will look nicer and bake more evenly. While not essential, a mandoline is an affordable kitchen tool worth the price.
10. Fill your tart shell with applesauce. Top with sliced apples and dust with cinnamon.
11. Bake at 350 degrees for 30-40 minutes.

Raspberry Galette

If you don't have a tart pan to make a shape like the previous recipe, you can make this rustic version instead. Simply roll the dough out the same way onto a silpat or dusted sheet pan, put your filling in the middle, and then fold the outer edges back in on the tart or "galette." This time I had fresh raspberries ripening by the barrel so I made a simple raspberry filling and topped that with more raspberries, dotting the whole thing with chocolate chips.

Regardless of how you shape your tart crust, remember that it can be filled with almost anything. From chicken pot pie to quiche and fruit tartlets, seasonal fruits with fruit puree, or custard filled with fresh fruit on top, it's hard to go wrong.

Ingredients:

1, 4 ounce tart dough disc(previous page)
4 cups raspberries or other fresh fruit
Sugar or honey/maple syrup to taste
1/2 cup semi sweet chocolate chips or callettes
2-4 tablespoons flour to thicken the filling

Directions:

1. Add your fruit to a saucepan starting with 1/4 cup of your sweetener
2. Cook for 5 to 10 minutes and taste to see if the sweetness or acidity needs any adjustment. Fruit varies not just from type to type, but also season to season, so use your taste buds
3. At this point, you also need to adjust the consistency so it won't be too wet. Start by taking one tablespoon of flour or cornstarch, dissolve it in a couple tablespoons of water, and add to the saucepan. Bring to a gentle simmer for a couple minutes to gel the starch.
4. If it is thick enough, allow to cool before filling your tart shell or galette
5. If it is still runny, repeat step 3 until desired thickness is achieved. Better to err on the side of too thick, as a wet filling will soften your crust
7. Roll out your crust into a circle about 1/8 inch thick
8. Put 1.5 cups of your filling in the center of your crust and spread a little, leaving room to fold your crust back over the filling
9. Fold the crust edges over your filling and put in a 350 degree oven for 30-40 minutes or until crust is golden brown and crispy

THE ANNUAL GRAIN SHARE DISTRIBUTION

Every January we hold our annual distribution event in Amherst and Boston, and sometimes even in Connecticut and New York. This is the perfect time to distribute grains and the most efficient and fun way to gather the annual grain harvest. Grain harvesting begins in late summer and continues into the fall, lasting to December in some cases Once the grain is harvested it needs to be cured (dried), sorted, and cleaned. By the time December comes, we know what we have to offer the membership and customization begins. Everyone gets their own customizing form online through a web link we send to members in mid-December. Each member chooses exactly what they would like their share to consist of.

Over the years, members come to know which varieties they love, how much of them they'll need to last the year It is a far more customizable experience than buying commodity grains from somewhere. Our grains and beans are not only higher quality than the commodity counterparts, but are consistently grown by the farmers using the same varieties so there is much less variation from year to year. This allows familiarity in addition to the connection of knowing where our food comes from and who grows it.

As the grain distribution has grown over the years, we have added new expansion shares like the Rice Share and The Farmer's Pantry Share. January and the remainder of the winter can be a tough time for locavores and foodies, but our annual distribution brings a whole new life and meaning to cooking and baking throughout the winter:

"When Ben started the PVGH CSA, we jumped at the opportunity to buy wheat that was locally grown. Now, we've experimented with the different varieties of wheat available from PVGH, and we have learned what our favorites are for biscuits, cookies, crumble, crusts, etc. The quality is phenomenal, and each year the distribution process has provided increased flexibility of choice.

Grain Types and Share Customizing

Each year there are over 25 different grain, flour, and bean options in the share. Members choose from a half share geared towards singles and couples (40-50lbs) or a whole share geared towards families (80-100lbs) and sign up during the growing season. Since this is designed to be a year's worth of grain, it works out to 1 pound per week for the half shares and 2 pounds per week for the full shares.

Members then receive a web link to their personal customizing page in mid-December to "build" their share from the selections available. With five types of wheat, four types of corn, three types of oats, four types of beans and rye, buckwheat, and the 7 types of flour available, there is a lot to choose from.

Wheat

- Einkorn
- Emmer
- Spelt
- Red Lammas

Beans

- Yellow Eye
- Jacob's Catlle
- Red Kidney
- Soldier Beans

Corn

- Popcorn
- Nothstine Dent
- Plymouth Flint
- Nothstine whole corn-meal flour

Oats

- Whole Groats
- Steel cut
- Rolled(not Steamed)

Other

- Buckwheat
- Rye
- Buckwheat flour
- Rye flour

All wheat is available as whole grain and as whole flour. There are two types available as sifted or "white flour;" however, since it is from stone milled wheat it has some germ and bran remaining in it and has a creamy color and delicious flavor.

Once members have made their selections, all the orders are compiled and I work with our six farms to get all the grains to our distribution locations for the big distribution every January and February. The Amherst area is always on the last Saturday in February and the Connecticut distribution is always on the last Sunday in January. The following weekend (the first Saturday in February) is always the Boston area distribution. These events have grown over the years and now serve over 400 shareholders each year. With continued growth and high member satisfaction, the shares keep getting better every year. There is nowhere else you can get so many grains of such high quality and value on the market for such a reasonable price. The incredible efficiency of the annual distribution combined with our dedicated farmers and flexible membership is what makes this possible.

CORN

Origins - History - Types - Qualities - Usage

Tlaoli(corn) - The Aztec Grass of Greatness

Tlaoli - First cultivated between 6,000 and 9,000 years ago from the wild grass Teosinte in Central America.

First domesticated in the Mexican highlands about 9,000 years ago, corn has become the most widely grown crop on the planet. It's wild predecessor, Teosinte,was a small grass with one finger sized cob towards the top that had eight rows of kernels. Though it originated from the highlands, it turned out to be one of the most adaptable crops ever cultivated and began spreading through South America six or seven thousand years ago, eventually reaching North America. Corn was the primary staple of the diet of the Aztecs, the Mayans, and the Incas. Corn has been cultivated in just about every size, color, and shape you can imagine and has similarly diverse potential in the kitchen.

When explorers from the Western Hemisphere arrived, corn was traded for and brought back to Europe. Despite fear of corn being low in nutrition, its adaptability and good taste would win out, and it would eventually be adopted by innumerable cultures around the world.

One thing that was lost was the tradition of nixtamalization that indigenous people of the Americas used to make corn softer and more nutritious, as well as remove potential poisonous aflatoxins from the outer layer of the kernel (nowadays our crops are carefully tested in laboratories to assure there are no myco-toxins to begin with). The Nahuatl word for this is nixtamal, or nix (meaning ash) and tamalli (meaning corn dough); ash was used as the alkaline substrate to soften the kernels with. This process gave corn incredible flavors and aromas of masa (another word for nixtamalized corn kernels) and made the Niacin nutritionally available, making it far more nutritious as a staple food. Tortillas, tamales, sopes, gorditas, atole, posole, and more are all made from a base of nixtamalized corn. While you can use ash to do this, I recommend using slaked lime instead, which should yield more consistent results. It also goes by the name of pickling lime and calcium oxide.

Types of Corn

Dent Corn - Developed in the mid 1800's and named for the little dent that forms at the top of the kernel, this type of "dry" or "grain" corn is the most common type of corn grown in the world. Used to make cornmeal, masa, polenta, johnny cakes, grits, and more

Flint Corn - An ancient corn grown by Native Americans dating back to before 1000 bc. It is used in a similar way that dent corn is, but it's harder in texture with less soft starch, hence the name "flint"

Popcorn - Archeological evidence for popcorn dates back to 3600 bc. It became very popular during the Great Depression after the steam-powered popping carts invented in the late 1890's made it cheap and widely available

Sweet Corn - With a very high sugar content, this type of corn also grown by Native Americans is best eaten fresh, not dried. This is the type you eat raw, or steam or boil like a vegetable

Flour Corn - Also a very ancient type of corn with a particularly soft starch and thin outer coating

Base Preparations

Masa

When a dry grain corn such as dent, flint, or flour corn is soaked and simmered in a solution of water and slaked lime (calcium hydroxide)

Nixtamalization

The name of the process of turning whole grain corn into masa corn

Cornmeal (corn flour)

Any type of grain corn ground into meal or flour

Grits

Cornmeal cooked with water into a creamy porridge

Polenta

Cornmeal cooked with water into a creamy porridge and then allowed to set as it is cooled. It is usually sliced and then fried, steamed, or baked

CHEESY GRITS AND CREAMY POLENTA

So simple and so comforting. Creamy and oozing when fresh out of the pot and then gelling into a sliceable form when cooled, allowing it to be fried or baked in slices. While this dish couldn't be simpler, the one danger is scorching the bottom as it cooks. It needs to simmer for at least 30 minutes to be fully cooked, so a heavy-bottomed pot and just enough heat to simmer slowly is the key. Alternatively, once brought to a simmer it can be finished in an oven at 350 degrees with no risk of scorching.

Once it is cooled, it can be returned to the creamy consistency by adding a little water or milk and stirring while reheating. Broiling cheese on top and adding bacon bits are always good moves and it makes an awesome accompaniment to almost any filet of fish or meat with a side of vegetables. The cooled sliced "cakes" can be dipped in egg batter and fried or baked and then drizzled with honey and butter.

Ingredients:

2 cups cornmeal
6 cups water
1 teaspoon salt

Directions:

1. Mix the cornmeal, salt, and water together in a heavy-bottomed pot and set on medium heat. The water must not be hot before mixing or the cornmeal will clump.
2. Bring to a gentle simmer, cover, and turn the heat to medium-low or even low. Do not omit the cover or it will scorch.
Alternatively, move to a preheated 350 degree oven once simmering
4. Simmer for 30 minutes.

If you follow these keys you'll always get perfect polenta with no scorching, no clumping, and very little work. The Nothstine dent corn is so flavorful that I like to keep the seasoning very simple. That way I can turn it into various dishes throughout the week.

One of the things that is so exceptional about polenta is its compatibility with so many flavors and dishes. It can simply be served as a delicious side with almost any meal, adding a creamy and luxurious counterpoint. It can be served under a piece of fish surrounded by a mushroom broth, topped with cheese, and broiled to a bubbling perfection, made into a casserole with seasonal vegetables and ricotta, or made into a quick satisfying breakfast with some maple syrup and a handful of toasted nuts and or some fruit.

SOUTHERN SKILLET CORNBREAD

WITH JALEPENOS, CHEDDAR AND BACON

This cornbread is the style of cornbread with no sugar and no wheat flour. Its crispy, crumbly texture goes incredibly well with savory foods like bacon and collards or chili con carne. You could make all three for an awesome feast!

The bacon and collards can be served on the side to accompany the cornbread or you can mix it into the batter for a souped up and portable cornbread meal. Alternatively, you can add things like jalapenos, cheddar , and bacon - feel free to be creative.

For the bacon and collards, you can pan fry the bacon first, leaving a tablespoon or two of bacon fat in the pan and reserving a couple tablespoons for the cornbread. Then rough chop your collards and add to the skillet, sauteing for 5-8 minutes and seasoning with 1/2 teaspoon of salt. Then move the collards into a preheated 350 degree oven, stirring occasionally. Cook the collards in the oven until they reach the perfect crispy, chewy texture, about 20-30 minutes. Cube the bacon stips and add to the collards to finish.

Ingredients:

2 cups or 9 ounces of Nothstine dent cornmeal(or plymouth flint)
1.5 cups buttermilk or whole milk and 2 tablespoons vinegar
2 large eggs
1 teaspoon baking soda
1/2 teaspoon baking powder
1 teaspoon salt
3 tablespoons butter
2 strips of bacon cookked and cubed
4 jalepenos with the seeds and pith removed

Directions:

1. Mix together dry ingredients in a large mixing bowl
2. Measure wet ingredients and stir into the dry mix
4. Stir in optional bacon and collard greens.
The consistency should be like cake batter. Thick but pourable. Adjust if necessary
4. Preheat oven to 400 degrees and rub your cast iron skillet (or baking dish) with butter coating. Pour batter in when your skillet starts to smoke a touch.
5. Place skillet in the oven and bake for 20-30 minutes until the batter is set (200 degrees or when a toothpick comes out clean
6. Allow to cool for ten minutes and then serve

Masa Corn
Nixtamal - Unlocking The Secret

Making nixtamal or masa corn is a simple and ancient technique to unlock the full nutrition and flavor from the corn. The whole corn kernels should simmer in a solution of water and pickling lime (aka alcium hydroxide) for 15-20 minutes, sit at room temperature for 24 hours and are then rinsed with cold water. This process softens the kernels, makes the niacin in the corn nutritionally available, and adds an incredible flavor to the corn. This is what most Native American food traditions on based on; from tortillas, sopes, and gorditas, to tamales, posole and atole, and many more, all these are made from "nixtamal."

Once the corn is transformed, it is usually ground into a dough with the addition of water and salt. A standard kitchen food processor works perfectly for this and is what I recommend to make your masa dough. To make the dough in the food processor, you'll want to use as little water as possible while allowing it to turn in the processor. The drier your masa dough is, the easier it will be to shape, especially if you're making thin tortillas. Sopes and gorditas can be shaped by hand while a tortilla press is best for making thin tortillas and are available at Mexican grocery stores or online for around 15 dollars.

The nixtamalized corn will keep well in the freezer for months and the masa dough will keep in your fridge for up to a week. I usually make a double batch and keep some masa in the freezer for another time.

Ingredients:

1 pound dry corn

1 Tablespoon Pickling lime(calcium oxide)

1 quart of water

Directions:

(for nixtamalization)

1. Mix together corn, water, and lime
2. Simmer for 15-20 minutes
3. Let stand at room temperature for about 24 hours
4. Pour into a colander and rinse thoroughly under cool running water

You now have nixtamalized corn or masa. This can be used in soups and stews (posole) or you can make it into a dough with your food processor and some water and salt to make tortillas, gorditas, sopes and more.

(to make masa dough)

1. Add 8 oz of masa kernels, ½ tsp of salt and 1/4-1/3 cup water into your food processor.
2. Process for several minutes, occasionally scraping the sides of your processor down to re-incorporate
3. You want to have just enough water to facilitate grinding so the dough becomes fairly smooth. Not enough water and it won't grind,too much water and it will be too wet to press out and handle easily.
4. You can always add more masa berries (or some cornmeal) or water to adjust consistency, but start easy on the water and only add more if necessary. You want a stiff, smooth clay like dough. If it is too sticky to easily pick up and handle, you need to add some more masa or a little cornmeal to get the stiff dough you'll need.
5. It will take 4-8 minutes to grind fully, taking care to not overheat the dough in the processor. Rest as needed. Once your dough is made, you are ready to pat out some gorditas, pinch a few sopes and press out your tortillas. If your dough is too sticky to handle, put it back into your food processor and add a little cornmeal to stiffen.

Gorditas, Sopes, and Tortillas

Starting from the easiest to the more challenging shapes, we'll start with gorditas, move on to sopes and then finish with tortillas.

Gordita means 'fat little tortilla' and is very easy to make and surprisingly wonderful to eat. You simply take a ball of dough about the size of a golf ball and pat it back and forth between your hands to form a flat 3-4 inch disc. I like to cook these in a pan or on a griddle with a little butter to give them a crispy outside and a creamy interior that is hard to beat. Eat straight away or dip into salsa, sour cream, or guacamole for a phenomenal treat.

Sopes start out as a gordita, but instead of griddling on both sides, the edges are pinched up on the sides to hold a filling/topping. Kind of like a tiny deep dish masa pizza. I like to griddle these for 3-5 minutes and then finish under the broiler to melt the toppings and finish cooking the sope through about 5 minutes under the broiler. You can top with bean and cheese, meats and cheese, or roasted veggies. Once they come out from the broiler, you can add salsa, guacamole or lettuce, scallions, herbs, etc.

While tortillas are not very difficult to make, it will probably take you a few tries to get the hang of it. A tortilla press is used with a thin piece of plastic folded between the press and your dough to peel off the tortilla after pressing. The most important factor is to make sure your dough is stiff enough to handle while staying very thin. Also, the dough is usually turned once or twice while pressing to even out any uneven spots. Once it is pressed to the desired size, the plastic is peeled back and the exposed side is flipped onto one hand. Then you peel the plastic off the other side and flip it right into a hot, dry pan.

TAMALES, POSOLE, AND ATOLE

Often made and served on New Year's Eve, Posole is the simplest use of masa corn, as the whole nixtamalized corn kernels are added to a soup or stew pot usually with pork, chiles, garlic, onions, and oregano, cumin, cilantro, and epazote (I highly recommend seeking out some epazote as it adds a wonderful special flavor). Sometimes beans are used in place of meat for a vegetarian version.

Tamales are made from masa dough that has some fat added. Usually, this is in the form of rendered pork lard, but bacon fat or butter can be used as well for a delicious result. Use 5-10 tablespoons of your choice fat and simply blend into your masa dough. While tamale dough can be baked in a casserole dish for tamale pie, it is traditionally wrapped in corn husks and steamed. Corn husks are soaked before filling and the tamale dough is spread onto the corn husk about 1/4 inch thick. Then a filling of cheese, stewed meat, or something sweet is put on top before it is rolled up, tied together and goes into a steamer for an hour.

Atole is the liquid form of masa. Often served as champurrado or chocolate atole, the base is masa blended with water, sugar, cinnamon, vanilla, and optional chocolate or fruit. Served warm, this filling beverage can be enjoyed anytime but is particularly comforting in cooler weather. While it can be made thin enough to drink, it is most often served thicker as a breakfast porridge or a warming afternoon snack.

FARMALL

FARMALL
130

BLUEBERRY CORN MUFFINS

These perfect little morning treats are as tasty as they are beautiful. The blueberries burst as they bake making moist little pockets of goodness.

Ingredients:

1.5 cups wheat flour
1/2 cup cornmeal
3/4 cup sugar
1 teaspoon baking soda
1 teaspoon baking powder
1 teaspoon salt
1 cup blueberries
2 large eggs
1 tablespoon lemon juice
Zest of 1 lemon
4 ounces butter(melted)
3/4 cup milk(or water)

Directions:

1. Pre heat your oven to 350 degrees.
2. Combine the dry ingredients in a large mixing bowl
3. In a smaller bowl whisk together the milk, melted butter, lemon juice, zest, and eggs
4. Fold the wet mix into the dry mix and add bluberries when 2/3 mixed
5. Scoop batter into a muffin pan lined with muffin liners 3/4 to the top.
6. Bake until set. Internal temperature should be 200 degrees. About 25-30 minutes

FOUNDATIONAL GRAINS OF CIVILIZATION

RICE

Origins - History - Types - Qualities - Usage

Domesticated in the Yangtzee River basin between 13,500 and 8,200 years ago rice from the wild rice Oryza rufipogon. By 4,500 years ago the two main species Japonica and Indica were in cultivation. Rice cultivation seems to have reached Korea and Japan by about 3,500 years ago bujt was not widely cultivated in permanent rice paddies for another 2-3,000 years. It now is consumed worldwide and accounts for about 19% of world human food consumption. While more wheat and corn is grown worldwide much of it goes to animal feed and ethanol production making rice the top for daily consumtion with wheat and corn in fairly close second and third respectively.

Of the three mostwidely consumed grains in the world(rice, wheat, and corn) rice is the simplest to prepare as it is mostly cooked as a whole grain and served with endless variety of curries, stir fries, chilis, stews, soups, sushi, etc., but is also used to prepare noodles, mochi, pudding and beverages(sake, rice milk and so on).

Rice is typically categorized by length and color but there are endless types and varieties making it difficult to generalize. But generally speaking longer rice tends to be less sticky and therefore stays more togther as whole kernels during cooking. However this is of course not always the case as in long grain Thai sticky rice. As with most grains the specific variety and the location and environment where it is grown as well as seasonal and fertility differences will create interesting and useful differences bewteen crops.

Here in New England we are only just beggining to experiment and grown rice on a commercial scale. The Varieties the Erik Grows in Vermont are medium-short grain varieties from Japan. The Seven Stars variety has been a delicious and versatile rice as it works well for sushi but is not so sticky that it can't be used for most other rice dishes. Hopefully over time we'll be able to grow more unique varieties here in New England as many are under trial with a good amount of success.

ERIC ANDRUS

GROWING METHODS: ORGANIC

Paddy Rice - Duck Aquaculture - Short Grain

Seven Stars Variety - White and Brown

SCP 21

Basic Rice Cooking Fundamentals

The simple preparation of rice is definitely one of the factors that has led to its importance in the human diet. Rice can be steamed or boiled until tender and served alone or with almost any accompaniment, side dish, or topping. However, it is worth learning a few tricks to get the most out of your rice.

1.Pre soak.

Soaking rice for 12-24 hours in cold water (or for 2 hours in warm water) will reduce cooking time almost by half and yield a more evenly-cooked and tastier result.

2. Cook ahead and let it rest.

Especially when making sushi, but in any case it is best to cook your rice ahead of time and let it rest for a little while after cooking (30 minutes to 2 hours). When you are serving or shaping the rice, it will be less delicate and easier to handle. It will also absorb sauces better and mix with other ingredients more readily.

3. Season your rice.

While rice can certainly be enjoyed totally plain, as with most foods it can easily be enhanced by various seasoning methods. Salt is the most basic seasoning, but adding kelp during cooking is common as well as using chicken stock as cooking liquid. A small dab of butter is also common in risotto which typically uses sweet white wine and chicken stock. And of course, rice vinegar with a little sugar and salt is the classic seasoned sushi rice preparation method, usually also combined with kelp.

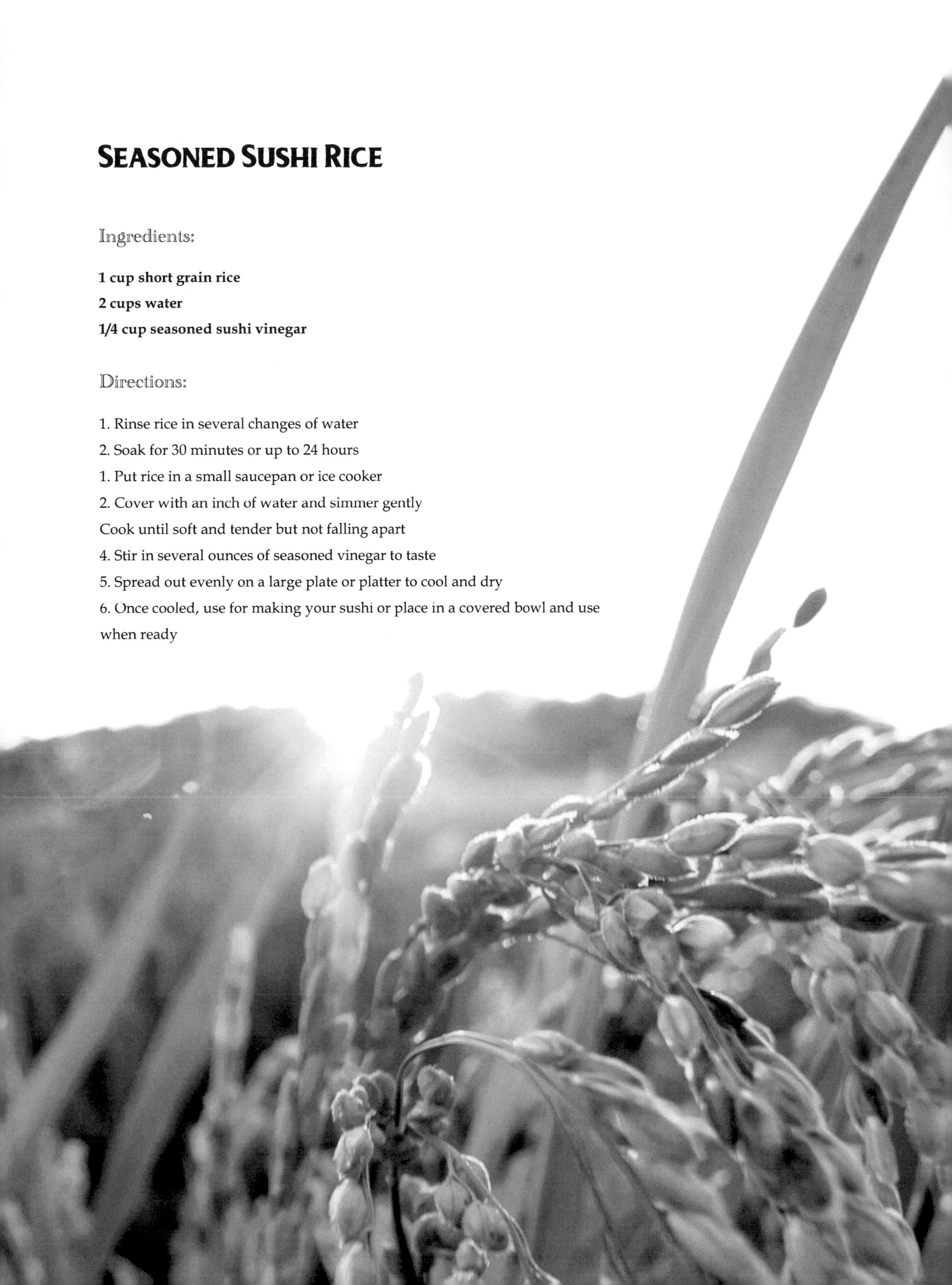

Seasoned Sushi Rice

Ingredients:

1 cup short grain rice

2 cups water

1/4 cup seasoned sushi vinegar

Directions:

1. Rinse rice in several changes of water
2. Soak for 30 minutes or up to 24 hours
1. Put rice in a small saucepan or ice cooker
2. Cover with an inch of water and simmer gently

Cook until soft and tender but not falling apart

4. Stir in several ounces of seasoned vinegar to taste
5. Spread out evenly on a large plate or platter to cool and dry
6. Once cooled, use for making your sushi or place in a covered bowl and use when ready

Sushi Nigiri and Maki

Soft shell crab "Maryland Roll"

Litle neck and soft shell steamer clams Gunkanmaki

Vegetable Maki and Nigiri Hototegai(scallop)

I had my first sushi when I was 14. What an incredible new world of food that opened up to me. By the time I was 20 I was no longer happy to be stuck eating sushi from restaurants. I had to learn this cuisine. While no one I knew made sushi at home, I wasn't going to let that stop me. Nothing a good bit of research and some trial and error couldn't solve. Initially I thought I'd be best off seeking tuna and salmon, but over time came to realize that the local seafood specialties were of course the best option for flavor, freshness, and affordability.

With the rice prepared a little ahead of time nothing is easier or more fun than rolling and pressing your delicious creations. While fresh and raw seafood is certainly the most popular, sushi is almost as versatile and boundless as pizza. From pickled vegetables to bacon and eggs (a personal favorite), you are limited only by your imagination, ingredients, and willingness to experiment.

SALMON, SCALLOP, AND KING CRAB NIGIRI AND SALMON, AVOCADO, AND CUCUMBER MAKI

THAI GREEN CURRY

WITH STICKY RICE, EGGPLANT, SUMMER SQUASH AND SNAP PEAS

This was one of the first things I ever tried to cook. My father moved to Waltham, MA when I was 18. There was a Thai restaurant called Tree Top and it was my introduction to Thai curries. The exotic flavors of lemongrass and kaffir lime leaves with the coconut and fish sauce entranced me. I had to try and make something this delicious. My first attempt was not so good. I had few of these ingredients at hand and still didn't understand the role salt played in preparing food. As I cooked and it tasted bland I added more and more spices. Of course it just became overly spicy while bland at the same time. Huh? But if anything it increased the mystique of these curries and while it was a little while before I tried again, it was the first time I was confronted with the fact that I needed to understand what the fundamental ingredients, techniques, and flavors were in order to recreate them at home. This was back before the internet was flooded with high-quality information on demand. Cookbooks had to be sought out and trips to the region sometimes were requisite if there were no well-made cookbooks on the regional cuisine. Nowadays it is absolutely incredible how many people all over the world are documenting and sharing their home and professional cuisines on the web, mostly through YouTube, blogs, and recipe sites.

Mark Wiens is of particular note, especially when it comes to Thai Cuisine. He is an American who is married to a Thai women and lives in Thailand with her family and their son. Not only does Mark share with you his mother-in-laws version of this Thai classic, but through his videos you can see an incredible variety of Thai techniques from all over the country. His focus on the ingredients and preparations takes you right into the kitchens to watch as these dishes are prepared while sharing his eating experience as well. It is incredibly informative and second only to being right there with him. I encourage you to find his channel and learn all about what is being cooked around the world. He is incredibly prolific and travels all over the world, documenting and sharing his experiences. There are also quite a few similar channels that cover areas from all over the world. Most notably, The Food Ranger and The Best Ever Food Review Show. The Latter being the most entertaining and probably my favorite if I had to choose.

Rice and curry paste form the basis for this dish while the vegetables, meat, or tofu can be swapped in or out depending on what you have on hand and what you're in the mood for. Chicken with eggplant, peppers, and green vegetables is traditional but you could easily go with tofu, shrimp, or any seafood, squash, carrots, green beans, ect. You can also use store bought green curry paste

Steamed Vegetables and Chicken

Ingredients:

2/3 cup green chiles
2 sticks lemongrass
3oz ginger
3oz galanghal
6 kaffir lime leaves
1 Head of garlic
1 shallot or half a medium onion
1 teaspoon Salt
1/4 teaspoon coriander, cumin and black pepper

1/2 pound chicken(or tofu, seafood, duck, beef, pork etc)
1 small eggplant
1 small summer squash
1/2 a medium onion
1 bell pepper
1 lime, zest and juice
1 tablespoon Fish sauce
Salt and pepper to taste
Scallions for garnish
10. 1/4 cup coconut cream

Directions:

1. Pierce your eggplant and set it to roast at 400 degrees until very soft all the way through. About 40 minutes.
2. Peel and chop your ingredients for the curry paste.
3. Blend in a blender, a food processor or use a mortar and pestle. Add water as needed to assist blending.
4. Freeze extra curry paste either in ice cube tray placed in freezer bags, or just lay flat in freezer bags.
5. Steam vegetables in a saute pan with a little water. Start with the vegetables that need the most cooking and add the rest as appropriate, including your protein.
6. Add curry paste, fish sauce, lime juice, and zest in the last 2 minutes of cooking and then finish with coconut cream as you take off the heat. Serve with rice and garnish with scallion or cilantro.

GUMBO AND RICE

My father discovered gumbo on a trip to New Orleans. It was probably my favorite dinner in my father's repertoire growing up. I believe it was also the start of my hot sauce addiction. My dad would have file powder and tabasco sauce at the table and while my taste for file had its limits, I discovered an ever growing craving for peppers, vinegar, and heat. As I grew accustomed to the heat, more hot sauce went in. Soon it was not hot at all. But the taste was equally addictive and at 9 it didn't occur to me to seek out hotter sauces, so my addiction went on pause. It wasn't until decades later that the allure of hot peppers would entrance me again. It was pretty amusing until I ran into a ghost pepper and couldn't see straight for 25 minutes. I still love it hot and peppery, but I'm not chasing anymore of those dragons.

Gumbo is a really unique stew featuring unusual flavors and textures from the browned roux to okra combined with sausage, seafood, and the holy trinity of creole cooking: bell peppers, onions, and celery. The Seven Stars rice works perfectly with gumbo (and just about anything, for that matter). Gumbo can be made in about an hour start to finish, but as with most stews it improves in flavor overnight. This recipe also makes a big pot, about 5 quarts. I like to put several quarts in the freezer for instant comfort food at any time.

As with most stews, it is meant to be a catch-all for the best of what's around. It can be made vegetarian or with just seafood or pork. Feature the vegetables and meats that you have around and you'll always have a hit.

Ingredients:

3 bell peppers
2 medium yellow onions
7 stalks of celery
4-6 cloves of garlic
4 cups chopped tomatoes
1/4 cup tomatoe paste
4 bay leaves
8 cups water
4 cups okra
12 ounces andoulie sausage
1 pound mixed seafood(crab, shrimp, squid, mussels, etc.)
2 teaspoons salt
1 teaspoon black pepper
1/2 teaspoon smoked paprika
1/3 cup wheat flour
1/3 cup vegetable oil

Directions:

1. Dice onions, bell peppers, and celery and saute or steam in the bottom of a large pot (5-8 quarts) for ten minutes
2. Meanwhile, slice the okra and sausage and set aside.
3. Add the tomatoes, chicken thighs, garlic, bay leaves, and tomato paste and simmer for ten minutes
4. Combine the flour and oil in a heavy-bottomed pan and cook on medium-high heat until well browned. Be careful not to burn...stir it the whole time while it is browning and don't take your eye off it.
5. Add the okra, water, and the roux and simmer for ten minutes
6. Put your rice on to simmer
7. Add the sausage and seafood and simmer for ten minutes
8. Season with 2 teaspoons salt and 1 teaspoon black pepper

FOUNDATIONAL LEGUMES OF CIVILIZATION

BEANS

Origins - History - Types - Qualities - Usage

Beans are one of the most important sources of protein and fiber for humanity today and historically. There are many types of beans: broad beans, lentils and chickpeas, mung beans, red beans, etc. We'll be covering the most common type of bean - phaseolus vulgaris, which aptly means "common bean".

Phaseolus Vulgaris has been grown in the Americas for thousands of years and was discovered by Europeans explorers when Columbus landed in the Bahamas and found the native populations growing them in fields. This is the type of bean famously grown in the "three sisters" planting technique where corn, squash, and beans are planted together in soil mounds to their mutual benefit. Varieties include kidney, Yellow eye, Jacob's Cattle, soldier (all in the share) as well as black, pinto, navy and cannellini.

Beans are true nutritional powerhouses and are more than worthy of making regular appearances on the dinner table. If you aren't familiar with the work of Doctor Michael Greger, allow me to introduce him. Author of the best selling "How Not To Die" and leading educator/researcher in the meta analysis of the scientific community's entire nutritional research body, there are few people more qualified to make nutritional recommendations for long life, lower disease risk, and improved quality of life. While he promotes many nutritional concepts, the consumption of whole grains and beans is very high on the list of key things to a healthy diet. "The most comprehensive analysis of diet and cancer ever performed was published by the American Institute for Cancer Research. Sifting through some half a million studies, nine independent research teams from around the globe created a landmark scientific consensus report reviewed by 21 of the top cancer researchers in the world." One of their summary cancer-prevention recommendations is to eat whole grains and/or legumes (beans, split peas, chickpeas, or lentils) with every meal. Not every week or every day. Every meal.

While beans are simple to prepare, they should be soaked before cooking so the final texture is smooth. The simplest thing to do is a 24-hour cold soak, but you can also pour boiling water over them 1-2 hours before cooking and get most of the same benefits. When beans are in their dry state they are probably the least perishable food you'll encounter, but once cooked they are significantly more prone to spoilage. Once cooked they should be eaten or refrigerated immediately to extend their shelf life. As long as they are cooled reasonably quickly, they should last about a week in your fridge. Sometimes I like to make a large batch and then freeze them in quart containers as they keep perfectly and indefinitely in that state.

Quick note on beans and farts: Research has shown that beans only increase flatulence in those who don't eat them regularly. So if you're worried about unwanted odours, just eat beans on the regular and your digestive system (and body) will thank you! Also research has shown that it flatulence is not affected by cooking method so don't fret...just cook!

Boston Baked Beans

This was a staple snack growing up in my household, although it was not something my father made from scratch. Canned Boston baked beans are tasty, but of course the homemade version always surpasses it. In colonial New England, baked beans were typically placed into brick ovens overnight as the heat slowly dissipated, along with brown bread or other slow cooking dishes.

You can make this entire dish in the time it takes your beans to cook because adding the seasoning takes only a couple minutes. If you soak your beans the day before your beans will cook in about an hour. Technically speaking I cook this on the stove top so it isn't actually baked, but you could bake it in your oven

Ingredients:

1lb(2.5 cups) yellow eye beans(any bean could work but yellow eye is my favorite for this as it holds shape well and has a sweet chestnut like flavor that is perfect
1/2 cup molasses
1/3 cup maple syrup
1/3 cup ketchup
1.5 tablespoons mustard
1.5 tablespoons onion powder or 1/3 cup diced onion
1 teaspoon salt
1/2 teaspoon black pepper
1/2 pound pork belly or bacon(optional)
1/2 pound kielbasa(optional)

Directions:

1. Soak your beans in 1.5 quarts cold water overnight or boil water and pour over beans 1-2 hours before cooking
2. Simmer beans gently for 30-90 minutes or until tender and smooth textured
3. Add the rest of the ingredients and stir to combine
4. Serve and enjoy!
5. If you are using pork belly into 1/2 inch cubes and saute until tender
6. Add pork belly and kielbasa and cook for 10-20 minutes to combine flavors

CHILI CON CARNE

This hearty warming stew originated in the 1800s in northern Mexico before it spread into Texas and further north. Originally it was prepared with dried beef, suet, chili peppers, and salt, pounded together and dried into bricks for traveling, cooked into a pot of boiling water. As chili parlors began serving hot chili con carne in the latter half of the 1800s, there was no reason to dry it into bricks and more combinations of ingredients became possible. Tomatoes and beans became common ingredients included in chilis and chili joints spread even further north, reaching Wisconsin by 1913 (and where you can still eat at the original Chili John's).

Chili can also be used to compliment other foods and have become classics unto themselves. From the chili dog, chili fries, and chili nachos to the New Mexican green chili (made with pork, green chilies, and tomatillos) and the vegetarian chilis that came with the vegetarian movement of the 1970s, there are endless possibilities.

So what chilis to use? There's no right or wrong answer, but I'll make some recommendations based on my personal preference and what is available in my area. For fresh chilis, I recommend poblanos for medium heat and fantastic flavor. If these are too hot for you or your family, the best lower heat options will probably be anaheim or cubanelle. For dried chilis, I recommend guajillo and pasilla, both with mild heat and excellent flavor. If you want to bring up the heat to higher levels, add just a few of the hotter peppers in addition to your base chilis. These include jalapeno, serrano, habanero, and chilis de arbol, to name a few. For a smoky touch without heat, use smoked paprika or use chipotles (smoked jalapenos) for some extra heat and smokiness.

Ingredients:

1 pound fresh mixed chilis or 4 ounces dried chilis,
or even better a mix.(1/2 lb and 2 ounces).
2 medium red onions
2 medium sized carrots
1 pound kidney or jacob's cattle beans
4 cups chopped tomatoes
4 cloves garlic
2 teaspoon salt
1 teaspoon black pepper
1/2 teaspoon cumin
1 tablespoon garlic powder
1 teaspoon dried oregano
1 pound ground beef
2 teaspoon salt
4 ounces tomato paste
Optional smoky and or hot chilis and chili powders

Directions:

1. Soak beans overnight in cold water or pour boiling water over beans and soak for 1-2 hours. Simmer until the beans are tender, drain and set aside
2. Destem your dried chilis and rough chop, removing pith and seeds for reduced heat.
3. Add tomatoes and chilis to your pot and bring to a simmer
4. Slice and add onions and carrots
5. De-seed fresh chilis (unless you want the extra heat), slice, and add to the pot
6. Add tomato paste, crushed garlic, salt, pepper, cumin, garlic powder, and dried oregano
7. Simmer gently for 1-3 hours depending on how chunky you like it. The longer you cook it, the more it will become one.
8. Add cooked beans
8. Add the ground beef at the end when you turn the heat off to avoid overcooking it

CASSOULET

WHITE BEAN, DUCK LEG AND PORK SAUSAGE STEW

Originating in southern france and named for the type of cooking vessel called a cassole, a deep earthenware pot, cassoulet is a simple country stew of white beans, duck leg, pork sausage and somtimes pork skin or other meats. It is common to use duck confit which is fine but it's better to cook the duck legs fresh. You can try to cook it all in one pot but the timing is diffiicult because bean cooking times are difficult to predict.

Ingredients:

1 pound Yellow eye beans
2 duck legs
12-16 ounces pork sausage
2 cups chopped tomatoes
2 medium onions
2 stalks celery
6 cloves of garlic
One bunch fresh thyme
Salt and pepper to taste

Directions:

1. Start your beans soaking the day before
2. Place your duck legs, tomatoes, onions, garlic, and celery in a eavy bottomed stew pot and simmer gently until the duck meat is falling off the bone. about 2 hours.
3. Cook your beans until tender and smooth in texture. 30-90 minutes
4. Add the cooked beans, fresh thyme(dried works too) and sliced sausage to the stew pot and season to taste.I prefer a smoked kielbasa but any sausage will work.
5. Add water or stock as necessary to adjust consistency and prevent scorching on the bottom.

STORAGE

Storing grains is very easy and almost fool-proof as long as you understand a few simple principles. First, I'll give some general recommendations and then we'll cover specific grain type considerations.

The first and most important consideration is temperature stability. The biggest cause of grain spoilage during storage is fluctuating temperatures. The simple solution to this is to keep your grains on the main level in your house where the temperature is mostly stable, ranging from 60-75 degrees. You should never store your grains in a garage, mudroom, attic, or unheated room. Drastic temperature from night to day temperatures will force moisture to move from the center of the grain to the surface, where mold will grow and spoil your grain. The best place for your grain is in your kitchen cupboards or a main level closet, if you need extra storage. Some people like to use their basement and while basement temperatures tend to be fairly stable, they are not ideal. Moisture levels tend to be very high in basements and mold tends to be very prevalent in these conditions. If you do store in the basement, I encourage you to use air sealed jars and not to open them in the basement where they will pick up moisture and mold spores.

The second most important consideration is containers and sealing. When a jar is properly sealed, neither moisture nor bugs can get in. Bugs can eat right through paper and plastic bags. The best type of storage containers are glass canning jars, like half-gallon and quart ball jars. They are cheap, durable, totally sealed, attractive, and reusable. They are quite tough and rarely ever break. They also don't scratch when cleaned, which in plastic creates places for mold and bugs to hide during cleaning. If you do go plastic, make sure you avoid snap type lids that don't tend to seal well - opt for a screw on lid instead. If you need to store a lot of one type of grain, you may want to use large bins that have a seal around their closure. The seals don't last forever, but they do keep bugs out for at least one season and then can be replaced.

The third best practice to employ is to buy a set of reusable, food grade desiccant packs and keep one per five pounds to a container. This really guarantees longer safer storage and should not be overlooked. They are cheap and easy to use and significantly extend storage life of your grains and flour.

If you use ball jars, desiccant packs, and keep your grain on a main floor in your house, you will never have a problem. If you follow these protocols and you do have a problem, I will be the first to gladly replace any grain shares that spoil.

With all that said, there are some exceptions specific to certain types of grains or flours that we'll go over here:

Beans - The least perishable of all. If they are stored properly they will last for years in your cupboards.

Whole small grains like wheat, rye and buckwheat - Will last at least one year under recommended storage conditions, but could probably last for a number of years. The only real worry here is pantry moths. As long as you notice pantry moths before they get out of hand, you can simply put the affected jar in your freezer for a week to kill any activity.

Corn, cornmeal, or corn flour - Actually the most perishable of grains. This is the only grain I recommend storing in your refrigerator or freezer at all times. It can be stored at room temperature with dessicant packs, but it may mold during the warm summer months if your house get warm. Be careful with corn.

Oats - Similar to most small grains, except that they are a bit more prone to mold, especially in the rolled form. Whole groats stored with dessicant packs should last 1-2 years at room temperature, but in a warm house, you may want to store them in the freezer or fridge during the summer months. Desiccant packs are key here. I have stored rolled oats for a year at room temperature with dessicant packs and have had no problems.

Flour from small grains like wheat, rye, and buckwheat - keep very well at a cool (60-70 degrees), stable room temperature as long as they are in an air sealed container with dessicant packs. This generally works from September through May. For warmer months it is best to move any flour into your refrigerator or freezer.

A few stand out notes on storage and containers:

- Temperature stability is critical. Never store grains in your garage, attic, or basement. A main floor of your house that stays between 60 and 75 degrees is essential
- Ball Jars with dessicant packs are the best option for for medium to long term storage
- Reusable desiccant packs are a cheap and simple way to greatly enhance storage life and quality of your grains and floursPlastic containers usually don't seal well enough to keep out pantry moths - ball jars do
- Corn and cornmeal should always be stored in your fridge or freezer
- Flour should be stored in the fridge or freezer during the summer months to avoid pantry moths

MILLING

History

The milling of grain has been going on for a very long time - with certainty at least 14,000 years but probably quite a bit longer, as stone tools have shown starch residue from grains dating back over 100,000 years.

The original method for milling grain was grinding berries between two stones, as is still done with the Mexican metate. In Europe it was more common to use a massive mortar and pestle called a "knocking stone".

Eventually kerning stones were invented - basically tiny gristmills where one stone turned on top of another and had a hole in the middle to feed grain. The top stone would be turned by hand and the grain would move down into the hole in the top stone and get crushed between the two. As flour accumulated, it would work its way out to the outer edge, just as in modern-day stone mills.

It was the invention of the roller mill in the 1800's that led to the most recent change in flour quality. Roller mills allowed nearly perfect separation of the bran, the germ, and the starchy endosperm. While this invention allowed "white flour" to be produced, which significantly improved shelf life, the consequences have been many. First and foremost, the nutritional value dropped so tremendously that both the United States and British governments began requiring the enrichment of wheat flour to prevent nutritional deficiency in mass populations.

Home Milling Today

Fortunately, today the options for milling at home are very diverse and often as simple as grinding your coffee beans. Most mills are electric powered, but hand cranked and even bicycle cranked mills are available as well. Back in the 1990's my father used an electric coffee burr mill to grind his specialty flours at home and some still do this today - the only drawback is that can make only 1 cup at a time.

Hand crank mill have a similar constraint - you can grind out about a cup in 5-10 minutes but try to mill 4 or 8 cups at a time and you'll have a problem...an hour later you'll still be there with a very sore arm.

Electric grain mills are the most practical option, and each year they get better, cheaper, and are available in more styles and sizes. I recommend two primary types and manufacturers. The best type of all-around home mill is the electric stone mills made in east Germany by the company Komo. They are reliable, fast, quiet, and easy to use on-the-go without slowing down the rest of your baking or cooking. They grind all grain types and last forever. The only downside is that it is the more expensive option up front.

The second type I recommend is an impact mill. The best of these is the Nutrimill, and at half the price of a Komo, can be a really good option. There are a couple downsides to the impact mill. As the name suggests, it is a higher speed mill and so it makes some dust puff around the mill as it grinds. It is also noisier, which isn't an issue for me, though it also sometimes has trouble with large corn kernels.

Flour available in the grain share

During the first 5 seasons, CSA only offered whole grains, but eventually our farms developed the capacity to mill their grain as well. There are typically 7 flours available in the share and they are all stone milled and mostly whole flours. Our stone ground wheat from Hardwick is also available in a sifted flour, but I would describe it as a creamy yellow flour, as it is neither white nor completely devoid of bran and germ.

THE FARMER'S PANTRY

During the years I ran Wheatberry, we sourced a lot of what we served and sold from local growers. In fact, all our meats and cheeses, most of our produce, and all of our "value added" farm products were sourced from local farms. When I closed the bakery, I wanted to keep supporting these local producers, as many of them were my friends and all were my community. We were also looking for ways to expand upon the success of the grain CSA, and it turned out that the annual distribution model that worked so well for grains could also be applied to "value added" products. Value added products are anything that has been grown on a farm that has been processed to add value. This includes fruit preserves, honey, dried mushrooms, seaweed, lacto fermented veggies, hot sauce, culinary herbs, tea blends, and ghee.

With 11 farms and 65 products to choose from, the Farmer's Pantry was an instant success. It is the perfect accompaniment to the grain share and brings so many special products all together in the same place. The farms and farmers we work with on this program are of exceptional quality and integrity, and having all this together in one place is a great connection in the local supply chain and community.

New products are developed every year by these farmers and often expand the offerings in the pantry share. This year, one of our members approached me about the soaps she has been making using some of the oats and cornmeal from the share as exfoliants. They will now be appearing in the available selections for the share!

My kitchen at home is filled with the products from the pantry share and I have to say they are incredible and inspiring quality. Below I will list the farmers and farms involved and what they offer in the pantry share, along with some commentary about how I like to use these delectable goodies.share with some commentary about how I like to use these delectable goodies.

Cheshire Garden -

I first met Patti and Ralph at the Greenfield Farmers Market in 2005 when they were our vendor neighbors. It was one of Wheatberry Bakery's first markets and they were one of our first customers. Their fruit preserves, herbal vinegars, and farmhouse mustards are second to none in the world. Their generosity of spirit and fun and lively way of things is always a joy. So glad to still be working with and connected to Patti and Ralph after all these years. Maintaining a connection to them was a big part of the inspiration for the Farmer's Pantry Share.

Warm Colors Apiary -

Another connection made at the Greenfield Farmers Market. Dan and Bonita not only make some of the best honey one will ever find, but they also have been teaching beekeeping to aspiring beekeepers for decades, making our region more honeylicious and bee-filled. Their raspberry flower, buckwheat flower, and apple blossom honeys are simply sensational.

Old Friends Farm -

Yet another relationship formed at that first Greenfield Farmers Market. Missy and Casey and the Old Friends Farm crew have been leading the way in ultra high quality produce and value added products for many years. It was their incredible salad greens that first stunned me. They were clearly raising the bar and other have had to follow suit since. Since then they have continued to add new production and products to their farm matrix. Pioneering ginger production in the Northeast led them to start making their award-winning ginger syrup and they have added to their phenomenal offerings since, including fresh and dried turmeric, dried ginger powder, chai tea blends, and some fantastic BBQ spice blends I use all the time.

Carr's Ciderhouse -

Nicole and Jonathan Blum not only run an incredible orchard here in Western MA, but make award-winning cider products. I always have their cider syrup at the ready to add incredible flavor and depth to sauces and dressings . Their cider vinegar is on another level and their cider switchels throwback to an earlier time. They are also Grain Share members and it's always fun and fulfilling when it goes both ways!

Fungi Ally -

Truly an ally to fungi and humans alike. Willie has been producing some of the finest fresh and dried mushrooms since 2013. Not only does Willie grow mushrooms, but he is seriously involved in educating others in the growing and production of mushrooms in the Northeast. Through SARE grants, online courses, and in-person workshops, Willie is leading the way to a healthier more integrated food system through fungi.

Larch Hanson (The Seaweed Man) -

Larch Hanson, also known as the Seaweed Man, has been wild harvesting seaweed off the coast of central Maine for over thirty years. Larch has also been teaching the craft to others in Maine for decades. If you've had wildcrafted seaweed from Maine, Larch is in some way responsible.

Full Kettle Farm -

I first met Greg Disterhoff at my bakery when he showed up with a beautiful crop of wheat many years ago. Since then he's become dedicated to the art and craft of raising mixed medicinal and culinary herbs on a one-acre parcel in Sunderland, MA. His herbal teas are second to none (except maybe Old Friends Farm chai tea blend). Grown by hand with love and care, his tea blends will breathe new life into your teapot, but I'll warn you...once you try them, there's no going back!

Hosta Hill -

Maddie Elling and Abe Hunrichs have been lacto fermenting local and regionally grown vegetables since 2011. When I first tasted their sauerkraut and kimchi, it was an aha moment. This was how vibrant and fresh lacto fermented veggies could taste when done with the best ingredients and careful artisanal production on a manageable scale.

The Kitchen Garden -

I first met Caroline Pam and Tim Wilcox at the Garlic and Arts Festival in 2006. Their vegetables looked perfect, but not in a uniform, industrial way. It looked like they had tended every heirloom vegetable with the utmost care and knowledge. Later we hosted a CSA drop off of theirs at Wheatberry, and eventually they started to produce their award-winning Sriracha from the fabulous hot peppers they had been growing. They also make a red and green salsa always have other products in the works. I hope they will add dry peppers and ground dried peppers to the mix, but only time will tell.

cider
vinegar
BATCH № 35
ciderhouse
cider
syrup
BATCH № 34
12.7 fluid oz.
OLD FRIENDS FARM
Ground Tumer
Net Weight: 0.4 oz
PO BOX 904 AMHERST, MA

Some of the beautiful faces behind the Farmer's Pantry Products from the top left going counter clockwise: Patti from Cheshire Gardens, Caroline from The KItchen Garden, Fungi Ally, Pattie's incredible preserves; Missy from Old Friends Farm with ginger, Abe and Maggie from Hosta Hill, Larch Hanson bringing in the seaweed, and my little cutie Ella who helped me with a Farmer's Pantry Product shoot drinking chai tea from Old Friends Farm.

HOSTA HILL
CHESHIRE GARDEN
The Mad Hatter's
Pepper Preserve
CHESHIRE GARDEN
King of Hearts
Strawberry Preserve
CHESHIRE GARDEN
Teddy Berry
Blackberry Preserve
Rosie's
Red Currant Preserve

FINAL THOUGHTS AND FUTURE PLANS

When I first read The French Laundry, Omnivore's Dilemma, and Kitchen Confidential nearly 20 years ago, I knew I was at the beginning of a long, exciting and challenging adventure. I dreamed that someday I would write a book that might inspire others to make great and small changes in their life for the better. I hope this book has reached you and nourished you and your life in some way, big or small.

Writing this book was a sizeable and somewhat intimidating project, but it turned out to be a really special and meaningful experience for me. To be able to capture so many years of work into one place (with no html constraints) has been a true joy. While I plan to spend the next 18-24 months doing workshops, talks and signings promoting the book as well as making video content to support and enrich what's in the book, I am also definitely planning to write another cookbook in the near future that will aim to expand and enrich these same topics.

As far as the Grain Share and annual distribution goes, we will continue to improve the current offerings as well as add new programs to the mix. We may also expand into some other areas of food distribution that work on the annual bulk distribution model.

If you made it this far in the book, I am guessing you got something out of it and that means the world to me. Please feel free to write me @ben@localgrain.org to share any of your experiences as they relate to this writing. I would love to hear from you.

Sincerely,

Benjamin Lester

KITCHEN NOTES:

The final 8 pages of this book are dedicated to your personal kitchen journey. It is a space to make notes and write recipes variations or new recipes altogether. You will find that the fineness of grind, relative humidity, and time of year has a significant impact on temperatures, timing, and hydration levels you'll need to adjust in your baking.

While I have done my best throughout the book to guide you,, now you will be able to note each time you deal with the seasonal and physical changes so you can refer to what you learned each time

Bake on...and take notes!

Made in the USA
Middletown, DE
30 January 2020